The

Quiltie Ladies

Garden Journal

THIS BOOK BELONGS TO

_____

VARIABLE STAR QUILTERS

Sallie Astheimer

Ann Chess

Jody Clemens

Nancy Coyle

Jan Deitcher

June Garges

Barb Garrett

Susan Goelz

Norma Grasse

Fay Ann Grider

Melissa Horn

Bev Musselman

Nancy Roan

Bertha Rush

Kathleen Shaw

Mary Shelly

Eleanor Shubert

All due care was exercised in compiling this book but we cannot be responsible for your interpretation of any portion.

Illustrated by: *Sally Astheimer and Melissa Horn*
Photographer: *Donald Roan*
3000 copies printed by Indian Valley Printing, Ltd., Souderton, PA.

Profits from this publication go towards charity.

For additional copies, send $19.95 per book plus $3.00 for postage, handling and taxes where applicable to:

Variable Star Quilters
16 Harbor Place
Souderton, PA 18964

WHO ARE THE QUILTIE LADIES?

After the completion of a quilting class at a local fabric store in 1977, the participants continued to meet. Enjoying each other's company, the group soon organized into a quilt club, the Variable Star Quilters. Monthly meetings at each other's homes for business, show and tell, support, nurturing, and especially lunch became routine. In 1996 they will have their eleventh quilt show. Proceeds are given to local charities.

⸻

They published The Quiltie Ladies Scrapbook in 1987. It contains a collection of quilt patterns, menus and recipes, and is now in its fifth printing. In 1990, the W.P.A. Museum Extension Quilt Project, a reprint of thirty of the original plates produced by the 1941 W.P.A. in South Langhorne, Pa., was reprinted by the Variable Star Quilters and General Resources Exchange in cooperation with the Reading Public Library.

⸻

The group received national acclaim in 1991 when they won the Grand Prize in a Museum of America Folk Art Contest. "Edith and Polly", winner of the Friends Sharing America contest, went on to tour the country and now resides at the museum in New York. Projects such as "J. Everitt and Friends (above)", inspired by a vintage photograph, exemplify the ability of the group to work together. A common interest in gardening, and a decade's accumulation of quilting ideas and recipes have led to the publication of this book.

⸻

As a group, the Variable Star Quilters have grown together while maintaining their quilting individually. With strong roots in tradition, each proceeds at her own pace down the path of creativity. In every activity each seems to find the job best suited for herself within her own level of expertise. This diversity is what bonds them together and offers support and inspiration.

⸻

QUILTS

On quilts...

Stars burst,

Vines swirl,

Designs come out,

Colors shine,

Memories return,

Best of all

Friendships begin to grow.

CHRISTIN GOELZ
AGE 9

1

2

3

4

5

6

7

8

9

10

...I enjoy flowers as much when they get old and dried out as when they were fresh. I don't know— I just look at those flowers, and in my mind, I still see the beauty they once had. I never throw any of them away.

VAN CLIBURN, BORN 1934

This can also be said for quilts.

THE QUILTIE LADIES

SNOW LADY©

Color the lady and her tree shades of white. Place her on a deep blue background and she'll appear frosty.

SNOW FLOWERS©

. . . .

NANCY ROAN
87" x 87"

Flowers are scarce when snow drifts cover the garden. Reminiscent of folded paper snowflakes of our childhood, these snowflowers "bloom" despite the weather.

11

12

13

14

15

16

17

18

19

20

...On Gardens and Quilts

My husband is a very good gardener. He says the secret of success is to "feed the soil, not the plant." I feel the same way about fabric and quilts:

I buy fabric to feed the collection, not a specific quilt. A rich selection of my favorite colors and prints close at hand helps my quilts grow and blossom.

MARSHA McCLOSKEY

SNOW FLOWERS©

FROST PICTURES

Frost pictures
On my pane;
Crystal castles
Silver rain.

Pearly gates
And snowy walls;
Lovely frozen
Waterfalls.

Hoary ferns
And shrubs and trees;
Clouds like shining
Fantasies.

Pages from a
Fairy book;
Every morning
Where I look.

OLIVER DRIVER

When the cold and blustry winds are whistling 'round the corners of the house, settle in by the fireside with a big bowl of this warming stew. Dream of your garden and all the quilts you want to make.

SEAFOOD STEW

4 cups fish stock or clam juice

1 bay leaf

2 cups dry white wine

1 teaspoon thyme

3 or 4 dashes Louisiana hot sauce

1 large onion, chopped

2 cloves garlic, chopped

1 sweet red pepper, thinly sliced

2 tablespoons olive oil

1 quart chopped tomatoes

Saute onion, pepper and garlic in olive oil but do not brown. Combine with broth, tomatoes, wine and seasoning. Simmer for $1/2$ hour.

Add: *2 dozen peeled and deveined shrimp*

1/2 pound scallops

1 pound crab meat

1 pound white fish cut into 1 inch cubes

Stir to heat but cook only until seafood is cooked. Discard bay leaf. Sprinkle with chopped parsley. Serves 8.

QUICK TOMATO HERB LOAF

3 cups flour

1 1/2 teaspoons baking powder

1 1/2 teaspoons baking soda

3/4 cup grated Parmesan cheese

2 tablespoons sugar

1 egg

1/4 cup oil

3 tablespoons minced parsley

2 teaspoons dried basil

1 15 ounce can pizza sauce

Combine dry ingredients and herbs in a bowl. Add combined liquid ingredients. Stir to blend well. Pour into greased 8 $1/2$" x 5" loaf pan. Bake at 350° for one hour or until it tests done. It may take longer.

A pear year, a dear year;
a cherry year, a merry year;
a plum year, a dumb year;

TRADITIONAL SAYING

FUSILLI SALAD

1/2 pound fusilli

1/2 pound sugar pod peas
   (parboil one minute)

1 bunch scallions, sliced

1/2 bunch broccoli
   (parboil one minute)

1 red sweet pepper cut in
   1/2" x 1/2" pieces

1 green sweet pepper cut in
   1/2" x 1/2" pieces

1/2 cup sliced water chestnuts

1/4 cup soy sauce

1 cup mayonnaise

1 pound cooked shrimp

1/2 cup frozen corn kernels (thawed)

1 tablespoon sesame oil

Black pepper

Dash of Tabasco sauce

Cook fusilli, drain, plunge into cold water
to cool. Drain. Toss with remaining
ingredients. Other pasta can be substituted.

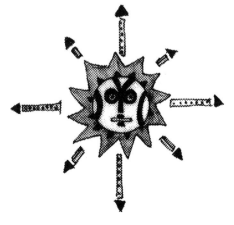

WARM CHERRY PUDDING

2 1/2 cups pitted sour pie cherries
   (not pie filling)

3/4 cup cherry juice

1/2 cup flour

1 1/4 cups sugar

1 tablespoon lemon juice

1/2 teaspoon almond extract

Cook juice, flour, sugar and lemon juice
until thickened. Add cherries and extract.
Cool.

TOPPING:

1 1/2 cups flour

1/2 teaspoon salt

1/2 teaspoon soda

1 cup brown sugar

3/4 cup oatmeal (flakes)

3/4 cup butter

Mix dry ingredients, cut in butter. Press 1/2
cup of the crumbs into the bottom of a 9"
ungreased cake pan. Spread with cherry
mixture. Top with remaining crumbs. Bake
at 375° for 30 minutes. Serve warm with
vanilla ice cream or whipped cream.

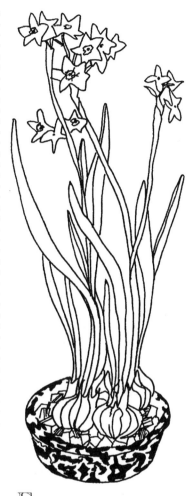

Fix a saucepan with water
and add spices such as cloves
or cinnamon and orange,
lemon or apple sections.

Simmer over a low heat
to add a wonderful scent
to the house.

Quilting is my therapy
for all disorders.

When quilting problems arise,
I've found great comfort
in turning to
my garden work.

HAZEL CARTER

21

22

23

24

25

26

27

28

29

30/31

> Announced by all the trumpets of the sky, Arrives the snow.
>
> RALPH WALDO EMERSON

OLD SNOWFLAKE

What color is a snowflake?
Yours may be blue,
mine may be silver.
Sometimes they are gray.
Just make it before it melts.

OLD SNOWFLAKE

BARBARA GARRETT
20" x 20"

Old snowflakes generally just
melt down to dingy gray along
the highway. We like this
example of vibrant colors better.

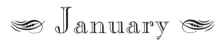

A SLEDDING PARTY

• **Bean and Pasta Soup**

• **A Good Sandwich**

Pickles
(from last summer's bounty)

• **Graham Cracker Brownies**

---

*N*o snow?
Come on.
You can think of some
excuse to have a party.
No snow?
As we prepared this
book, we experienced the
deepest snowfall in
decades, over 30 inches,
which was quickly
dubbed the
"Blizzard of '96."

*F*or an excellent fertilizer
for African Violets,
dissolve 1 tablespoon
Epsom salts in 1 pint
of warm water, then cool
to room temperature.

BEAN AND PASTA SOUP

6 slices bacon, chopped

1 cup onion, chopped

1/2 cup celery chopped

1/2 cup carrot, chopped

1 28 ounce can crushed tomatoes

2 15-1/2 ounce cans white beans, drained

*3 13-3/4 ounce cans low sodium
    chicken broth*

1/2 teaspoon black pepper

1 1/4 cups small pasta

1/4 teaspoons thyme

Fry bacon until almost crisp, drain and set
aside. Rescue a tablespoon of the fat. Sauté
onion, celery and carrot until soft. Add
remaining ingredients, simmer until pasta is
done. Add bacon before serving.

MUSTARD CHEESE PRETZEL DIP

*1 cup soft processed cheddar
    cheese spread*

3 tablespoons brown mustard

1 tablespoon sweet hot mustard

1 teaspoon horseradish

1 tablespoon red wine vinegar

Combine all ingredients. Pack into a crock.
Serve with pretzels. Adjust seasoning to suit
your own taste. This is quite mustardy.

A GOOD SANDWICH

Slice 5 or 6 slices of Italian bread on the
diagonal. Butter slices and brown on a
griddle or in a heavy fry pan. Remove from
heat but leave bread in pan. Top with thinly
sliced baked ham and some of the following
mixture:

1 cup shredded cheddar cheese

2 tablespoons finely chopped onion

1 tablespoon horseradish

1 teaspoon prepared mustard

1 egg

2 tablespoons chopped parsley

Spread on ham and broil till bubbly.

GRAHAM CRACKER BROWNIES

2 cups graham cracker crumbs

1 can sweetened condensed milk

1 cup chocolate chips

1 cup broken walnuts (optional)

Pinch of salt

1 teaspoon vanilla

Mix ingredients in bowl and press into greased 8 ¹/₂" square pan. Bake 25 minutes at 350°.

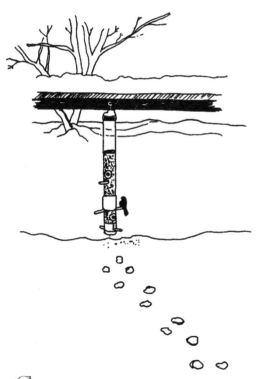

Cover any metal perches of bird feeders with masking tape so that the bird's feet don't stick to the perches in frigid weather.

WILD BIRD SEED

1 ³/₄ cups peanut butter
(chunky is great)

1 pound lard or fat from cooking

3 ¹/₂ cups rolled oats plus
2 additional cups

3 ¹/₂ cups cream of wheat

3 ¹/₂ cups cornmeal

4 cups water

Combine 3 ¹/₂ cups rolled oats with remaining ingredients except water and mix as best as you can to distribute the peanut butter. Bring water to a boil and stir in the 2 cups rolled oats, let mixture return to a boil and cook 2 minutes. Remove from heat and pout over peanut butter mix. You may need to get in there with your hands. Add sunflower seeds or nut meats to embellish the mix. This makes a lot but freezes well. Shape into desired form before freezing. Our bird watcher friend Joanne shaped the mixture into balls, and placed them in recycled egg cartons to freeze. She uses these balls in a suet log holder.

Much loved by most birds especially chickadees, titmice, woodpeckers, and Carolina wrens, even orioles and catbirds in the spring.

In designing a camouflage for a garden area, avoid using plants of striking shape or color as they will draw attention to the sight instead of concealing it from the viewer.

LEE'S PRETZELS

*Broken pieces of thick
  pretzels*

1 cup oil

1 teaspoon dill

1 teaspoon lemon & pepper

1/2 teaspoon garlic salt

*1 packet Hidden Valley
  Ranch dressing mix*

Bake at 350° for 10 minutes,
shake around, bake another
10 minutes.

1

2

3

4

5

6

7

8

9

10

Much February
snow
A fine summer cloth
show

TRADITIONAL RHYME

Plan a child's
garden. Children
love to touch, smell,
and pick the flowers.
Remember to include
lambs ear which is
so soft to touch.

Sunflowers produce
such magnificence
from a single seed.

Do not make the
mistake of trying to
rush the season by
planting too much
too soon inside. If
you do you will have
crowded and spindly
plants.

FORGET ME NOT

. . . .

MELISSA HORN
45" X 57"

This romantic Valentine quilt is reminiscent of an old fashioned Victorian token of affection. Note how the cut out areas give it a "lacy" effect.

❧ February ❧

GROUND HOG DAY SUPPER

· · · ·

• **Sausage Corn Chowder**

• **Focaccia**

• **Apple Cake**
with
Ice Cream
and
• **Hot Caramel Sauce**

February 2 is Ground Hog Day. Serve sausage (ground hog) and consider the ground hog's prediction. However, spring will come in spite of him. If his prediction indicates an early spring get on to garden planning. If not, keep on quilting.

SAUSAGE CORN CHOWDER
· · · · · · · · ·

1 large onion finely chopped

4 garlic cloves, finely chopped

1 tablespoon olive oil

1 lb. Italian Sausage (Hot or Mild)

2 cups of corn

4 cups of milk or half and half

2 cups of chicken broth

1/2 teaspoon cumin

2 tablespoons flour

2 large potatoes, diced

1 bay leaf

1 tablespoon chopped chili peppers

Sauté onion and garlic in olive oil. Cook potatoes in chicken broth. Slice sausage and sauté until browned, drain and discard fat.

Combine all the ingredients except flour, simmer for 10-15 minutes. Remove bay leaf, thicken with the flour. Check for seasoning and add salt and pepper if needed.

FOCACCIA
· · · · · ·

1 package dry yeast

1 tablespoon sugar

1 teaspoon salt

3 cups flour

1 cup warm water

1/4 cup olive oil

Combine first five ingredients in a bowl. Add water and oil and mix to make a soft dough. Knead until smooth. Let rise 1 1/2 hours. Pat into a greased 9" x 9" pan. Let rise 1/2 hour. Brush with 1 tablespoon of oil. Sprinkle with course salt, finely chopped red onion and chopped rosemary. Bake at 450° for about 40 minutes until nicely browned.

APPLE CAKE

1 1/2 cups oil
1 cup white sugar
1 cup brown sugar
3 eggs
2 teaspoons vanilla

Combine and beat until well blended.

3 cups flour
1 teaspoon baking soda
1/2 teaspoon baking powder
1 teaspoon cinnamon
1 teaspoon nutmeg
1 tablespoon orange rind
1 cup chopped pecans
4 cups chopped apples

Combine and add to oil, eggs and sugar.

Pour into a well greased tube pan, bake at
325° degrees for 1 hour and 15 minutes.
Serve with vanilla or butter pecan ice cream
and hot caramel sauce.

HOT CARAMEL SAUCE

1/2 cup sugar
1/2 cup brown sugar
1/2 cup heavy cream
1/2 cup butter
2 tablespoons rum

Combine and heat over low heat.

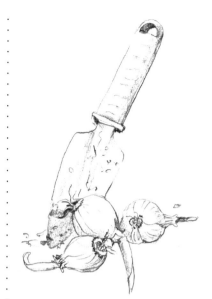

Pick color themes for your
garden tools and your quilt.
Clean and paint your tool
handles; pink, purple, yellow
or orange so that you can find
them in the garden.
Then to the fabric store.

CRIMSON ROSE VALENTINE

Take advantage of the center patch to pen an endearing sentiment, then choose the colors you love to complete your valentine.

Lovage root in the bath water will make you more lovable.

Put mugwort into your pillow to have dreams that reveal your future.

11

12

Flowers leave some of their fragrance in the hand that bestows them.

CHINESE PROVERB

13

14

15

16

17

18

19

20

VALENTINE TOPIARY

A Fantasy in Broderie Perse

**AUTOGRAPH BOOK OF
CHARLES MERTZ**

· · · · · · · · · · ·

JULY 20, 1886

· · · · · ·

To Charlie

There is a little flower
that blooms on yonder spot.
It whispers all I have to say
Which is forget me not

*Your cousin,
Emily R. Sterner*

VALENTINE LUNCHEON

- **Mushroom Onion Soup**

- **Chicken Romaine Salad**
  with
  Honey Mustard Dressing

- **Vanilla Frozen Custard**

- **Hot Caramel Sauce**

Winter blahs and blizzards getting you down?

Invite a bunch of lovers to lunch - quilt lovers, that is. Talking about quilts will dispel the cold and revive your spirits.

MUSHROOM ONION SOUP

2 cups fresh mushrooms

3 tablespoons butter or margarine

2 medium onions, chopped

2 tablespoons flour

5 cups chicken broth

1/2 teaspoon salt and a dash of pepper

1/3 cup uncooked rice

1 bay leaf

2 tablespoons chopped fresh parsley

Trim mushroom stems level with caps. Finely chop stems & thinly slice caps. In a large saucepan, melt butter, add mushrooms and onions. Cook and stir over low heat for five minutes. Blend in flour, add broth, salt and pepper. Cook, stirring constantly, until mixture boils. Reduce heat. Add rice and bay leaf, cover & simmer 15-20 minutes, until rice is tender. Discard bay leaf. Sprinkle with parsley.

Yield: 4 servings

CHICKEN ROMAINE SALAD WITH HONEY MUSTARD DRESSING

Flatten skinless and boneless chicken breasts and sauté until lightly browned and thoroughly cooked in a mixture of oil and butter with a clove of garlic. Season with salt and pepper. Cool. Do not chill unless the salad will not be served soon.

MAKE A SALAD BY LAYERING:

Shredded Romaine

Shredded Jack cheese (or Cooper sharp)

Chopped seeded & peeled tomato

Sliced fresh mushrooms

Crumbled cooked bacon

Sliced Chicken (above)

DRESSING

3 tablespoons red wine vinegar

3 tablespoons honey

Heat to melt honey. When cool, add:

6 tablespoons mayonnaise

1 tablespoon mustard

1 tablespoon finely chopped onion

3/4 cup salad oil

Vanilla Frozen Custard

4 egg yolks

¹/₂ cup sugar

¹/₂ cup milk

2 cups whipping cream

2 teaspoons vanilla

1 tablespoon rum

Beat egg yolks and sugar until light. Add milk. Cook in double boiler to 160° degrees, or cook in microwave. Do not overcook. Pour into a bowl and cover with plastic wrap and chill. Whip cream with vanilla and rum. Fold a portion of whipped cream into the cooled custard then fold in the remaining whipped cream. Spoon into a bread pan lined with plastic wrap. Cover and freeze. Slice to serve. Drizzle servings with Hot Caramel Sauce from page 13.

Quilting-Yes, Gardening-No.

My cultivation energy is put to cloth rather than dirt. But I do spend time praising my husband who tends to the yard. When we first moved to Hendersonville, before quilting, I kept a garden at Connemara, the Carl Sandburg home.

Soon, I discovered the money I was saving on growing our vegetables was spent on gas for the car going and coming from the garden.

However, I did learn how brussel sprouts grow!

Georgia J. Bonesteel

Bleeding Heart

Burgundy, pinks, rose and a touch of somber gray.

Where Rosemary flourishes, the lady rules.

I wish I was a little seed, I'd grow an grow an grow I'd twine myself around your heart and never let you go.

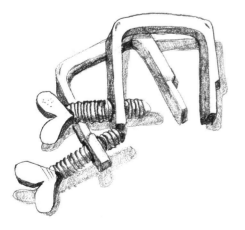

SHRIMP BUTTER HEARTS
· · · ·

¹/₄ lb. butter, softened

8 oz. cream cheese, softened

1 teaspoon lemon juice

4 tablespoons mayonnaise

Rind of small lemon, grated

1 6-oz. can of small shrimp, chopped fine

¹/₄ teaspoon garlic salt

Dash of pepper

Mix together until thoroughly blended. Spread on wax paper to ¹/₂" thick. Chill thoroughly. Cut into desired shape with cookie cutter. Hearts are just the thing for Valentines Day. Serve with crackers as an hors d'oeuvre.

Plain butter shapes coordinated with the season or an event add interest to the dinner table. Turkeys for Thanksgiving, stars for Christmas, butterflies for a Garden Party, are a few suggestions.

21

22

23

24

25

26

27

28

29

A sprig of thyme, a sprig of rosemary, one in each shoe, promises a girl that she will dream of her beloved.

WINDBLOWN TULIPS

. . . .

ELEANOR SHUBERT
76" x 77"

To see tulips tossed by springtime breezes gives promise of winter's demise. On this quilt the red tulips add sparkle to the dazzle, hastening summer's warmth.

WINDBLOWN TULIP

My garden will never
make me famous,

I'm a horticultural ignoramus.

I can't tell a string bean
from a soybean,

Or even a girl bean
from a boy bean.

OGDEN NASH

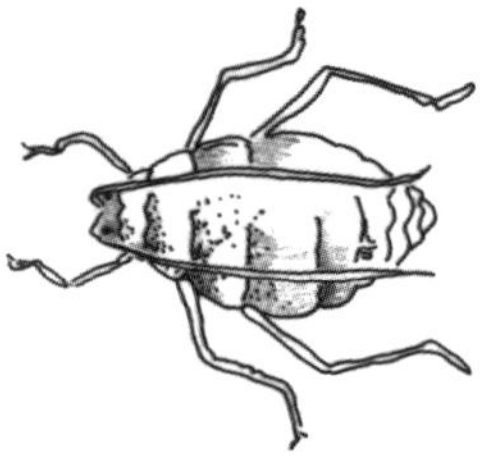

1

2

Mist in March,
frost in May

TRADITIONAL SAYING

3

4

5

6

7

8

9

10

CHICKEN PUFFS

3 oz. softened cream cheese

2 tablespoons soft butter

2 cups cubed cooked chicken

1/4 teaspoon salt

1/8 teaspoon pepper

2 tablespoons milk

1 tablespoon chopped chives

1 tablespoon chopped pimento

8 oz. can crescent rolls

Melted butter

3/4 cup crushed seasoned croutons

Blend butter into cream cheese until smooth. Mix in chicken, salt, pepper, milk, chives, and pimento. Separate crescent rolls into 4 rectangles and seal perforations. Spoon 1/2 cup chicken mixture onto center of each rectangle. Pull the four corners of the dough to center over chicken and seal. Brush tops with melted butter, dip in crushed croutons. Bake crumb side up on ungreased cookie sheet at 350° for 20 to 25 minutes or until golden brown.

MUSHROOM MOUSSELINE

1 lb. mushrooms

4 tablespoons butter

3 eggs

3 tablespoons heavy cream

*Pinch of salt, pepper, nutmeg;
    some tarragon (optional)*

Prepare and wash the mushrooms, sauté them in butter with salt and pepper, then mash them (or grind). Add the eggs, one at a time stirring well, then the cream, nutmeg and tarragon.

Grease a soufflé dish. Put in the mushroom mixture. Put the dish in a bigger one filled with water. Bake at 300°– 350° for 25 minutes.

While it's cooking, prepare a white sauce with:

3 tablespoons butter

4 tablespoons flour

1/2 cup chicken broth

1/2 cup milk

Salt, pepper

Unmold, cut into wedges, pour the sauce over it and decorate with chives. Present it on lettuce.

Serves 4-6.

CELEBRATE SPRING

- **Chicken Puffs**

- **Mushroom Mousseline**

King Size Green Salad
with
Vinaigrette

- **Bellefonte Cake**

Fickle March weather might not invoke feelings of springtime, but then again warm breezes may be urging the crocus and early jonquil to make an appearance. Then you'll know spring is truly on its way. Buy a bunch of daffodils to improve your mood.

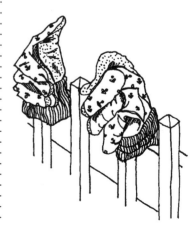

Lay your patio bricks in a quilt pattern - Court house steps works well. Lay a sample repeat pattern, measure, then stretch string base material in a grid - with one square equal to the measurement of the pattern, repeat. This simplifies alignment of the rows of bricks. Use 2" decorative block for the center.

GARDEN GLOVES©

MELISSA HORN AND
NANCY ROAN
28" x 28"

Perfect lollipop flowers and pure white garden gloves are easily achieved by the quilter. Gardeners usually have to settle for something less.

BELLEFONTE CAKE

1 box yellow cake mix

Juice drained from 1 10-ounce can of mandarin orange slices.

1 stick butter

4 eggs

Mandarin orange slices

Combine first 4 ingredients and beat until well blended. Stir in mandarin orange slices. Pour into 3 greased and floured 8" square pans. Bake at 350° for 25 minutes. Let cakes cool completely. Remove from pans. Ice with the following:

1 12 ounce cool whip

1 package instant vanilla pudding

1 20 ounce can of crushed pineapple, well drained

Best if made a day or two before serving. Refrigerate.

EASTER EGGS

Save the brown skins from onions all winter.

Line a pot with onion skins, place eggs in pot and add more onion skins pushing them between eggs. Cover with water and cook for at least a half hour. The more onion skins the deeper the color. Remove eggs and cool.

The Pennsylvania Germans scratch designs and dates on onion skin dyed eggs. If kept cool and dry the eggs keep for a long time. Examples in museums date back to the 1800's.

11

12

13

14

15

16

17

18

19

20

I can enjoy flowers quite happily without translating them into Latin. I can even pick them with success and pleasure. What, frankly I can't do is arrange them.

CORNELIA OTIS
SKINNER
(1901-1979)

"Sanst Gertraut
Plantz Kraut"

FOLK RHYME
USED TO HELP
REMEMBER TO
PLANT THE
SPRING GARDEN
ON MARCH 17.

GARDEN GLOVES©

Reduce the weight of large planters-fill the bottom two thirds with aluminum cans before adding soil. Place an old window screen in between the layers for easier dirt removal later. Makes moving planters more manageable.

A TRIBUTE TO ST. GERTRUDE

. . . . .

- Layered Cabbage Casserole

Crusty Seeded Rye Bread

- Marble Ricotta Cake

March 17 is also St. Gertrude's Day and was the day when the old Pennsylvania Germans sowed cabbage seeds. Pay tribute to Gert and serve this tasty cabbage dish.

LAYERED CABBAGE CASSEROLE

¹/₂ cup cooked rice

6 to 8 slices bacon

1 cup onion, chopped

2 cloves garlic, chopped

¹/₂ lb. bulk sausage or ground beef

¹/₂ lb. kielbasa, sliced

1 tablespoon paprika

2 cups sauerkraut

8 ounces seasoned tomato sauce

1 cup sour cream

¹/₄ cup milk

1 egg, beaten

2 tablespoons onion, finely chopped

Fry bacon until almost crisp. Break into small pieces. Sauté onions and garlic in bacon fat until limp. Add sausage or ground beef and cook until no longer pink. Add kielbasa, paprika, and cook to heat thoroughly. Place half of the sauerkraut in a well-greased casserole, then half of the meat mixture, the rice, then the remaining meat, and finally the remaining sauerkraut. Sprinkle with bacon. Spread the tomato sauce over the top. Combine sour cream, chopped onion, milk, and egg, then spread on top of tomato sauce. Bake at 350° for one hour.

MARBLE RICOTTA CAKE

1 18 ¹/₄ ounce box of marble cake mix: Mix as directed on box. Spread in 9" x 13" pan.

Mix the next four ingredients

2 lbs. ricotta cheese

4 eggs

³/₄ cup sugar

1 teaspoon vanilla

Mix and spread on top of prepared cake batter. Bake at 350° for one hour. Cool.

TOPPING

. . .

Mix one small box instant chocolate pudding, one cup milk, 8 ounces cool whip. Spread on top and refrigerate.

SAUERKRAUT CANDY

Don't Panic - there is no sauerkraut in this recipe, the coconut just looks like sauerkraut.

2 cups light brown sugar

2 cups granulated sugar

1 1/4 cups half and half

1/4 cup light corn syrup

1/4 cup butter

1 1/2 teaspoons vanilla

1 1/4 cups coconut

Combine the sugars, half and half, and corn syrup in a heavy saucepan. Cook over moderate heat until sugar is dissolved. Wipe sides of pan with a wet brush to remove any sugar crystals. Increase heat and cook without stirring to 250° degrees. Remove from heat, stir in the butter, vanilla and the coconut. Pour into a buttered 8" x 8" pan. Spread the candy with an oiled knife into 1 1/2 inch pieces. Let cool and cut along scored marks. Wrap in wax paper. Store in a tight container.

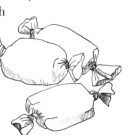

To make a lightweight cast concrete for garden sculptures, or troughs or planters, combine the following:

1 1/2 parts peat moss

1 1/2 parts garden vermiculile or perlite

1 part portland cement

Mix with water to desired consistency, let air dry.

Bright little buttercup, now will you show

Whether my darling likes butter or no.

Buttercup, buttercup, will you begin?

Shine me an answer under her chin.

Blossom by blossom the spring begins

ALGERNON SWINBURNE
(1837-1909)

SPRING CROCUS©

Check the bulb catalogue and color accordingly. Make one of each shade.

Remove your winter mulch in stages to allow the soil to warm slowly and not "heave" your perennials out of the soil.

21

22

23

24

25

26

27

28

29

30/31

There was an old
weather-vane
high on a shed,

The wind came a courting
and turned his head;

And all it could utter for
lack of a mouth

Was—East, and West,
and North,
and South.

BABY TULIP

BABY TULIPS

BARBARA GARRETT
18" x 18"

Form and color give this
doll-size quilt a charming
folk quality.

1

2

3

4

5

6

7

8

9

10

U*se a Post-it
stick for paste up of
fabric samples when
planning a quilt.
You can peel off and
reposition if you
change your mind.*

A*pril's anger is
swift to fall,
April's wonder is
worth it all.*

SIR HENRY
NEWBOLT

O*'er folded blooms
On swirls of musk,
the beetle booms a
down the glooms
And bumps along
the dusk.*

JANE WHITECOMB
RILEY
1849-1916

GARDEN TRADITIONS

BERTHA RUSH
72" x 86"

Selecting motifs from several sources provided an assortment of garden inspired motifs for this quilt. It gives the illusion we could walk up the gravel right into the garden.

INCOME TAX DAY INDULGENCE

- Pork Tenderloin Dijon
- Potato Cups
- Baked Onions Au Gratin
- Warm Raspberry Salad
- Mad about Chocolate Cake

You've paid your due to Uncle Sam, now do something nice for yourself. Indulge in this elegant dinner, then go out for the evening and buy several yards of that fabric you've been hankering for.

PORK TENDERLOIN DIJON

2 boneless pork tenderloins
2 tablespoons Dijon mustard
2 finely minced garlic cloves
2 tablespoons lemon juice

Grill tenderloins until about half done. Combine the mustard, garlic, and lemon juice into a paste, then brush tenderloins with mustard paste and finish cooking. Turn and brush with more sauce. Watch carefully and keep heat low so they do not burn. Can also be done in the oven.

POTATO CUPS

3 pounds potatoes, peeled
Rich chicken broth
Butter
1 medium onion, very finely chopped
1 clove of garlic, minced
1/2 cup of parsley, minced

Cut up potatoes and cook in lightly salted water until tender. Mash, add chicken stock to make mashed potatoes of medium consistency. Puree onion and garlic and sauté in butter until cooked and browned slightly. Add to potato mixture, season with salt and pepper to taste. Add parsley. Spoon into well greased custard cups, dot with additional butter if desired. Sprinkle with paprika and bake until hot.

BAKED ONIONS AU GRATIN

8 medium yellow onions, peeled and sliced
2 tablespoons butter
1/4 cup dry cocktail sherry
1/8 teaspoon nutmeg
Salt and pepper to taste
1/4 cup heavy cream
1/2 cup grated Swiss cheese
1/4 cup grated Parmesan cheese

In two batches, sauté the onions in the butter, in a large frying pan. Cook only until limp. Do not brown or discolor. Deglaze the pan, or remove the onions from the pan and pour sherry, scraping the pan with a wooden spoon to dissolve the brown toasted onion.

Mix the onions, the sherry, nutmeg, salt, pepper and heavy cream together and place in a baking dish. Top with the Swiss Cheese and then the Parmesan. Bake at 375° until top is a bit brown and bubbling. 15 to 20 minutes. Serves 8

WARM RASPBERRY SALAD

Large bowl of mixed greens

2 tablespoons olive oil

1/2 cup slivered almonds

1 1/2 cups sliced mushrooms

1/4 cup red wine vinegar

*2 tablespoons raspberry juice, drained
    from frozen berries or crushed fresh*

1 cup fresh or frozen raspberries

Heat oil in a fry pan. Sauté almonds until lightly browned. Add mushrooms and sauté for a few minutes. Add vinegar and raspberry juice, bring to a boil. Pour over greens, toss in berries and serve immediately.

MAD ABOUT CHOCOLATE CAKE

1 cup boiling water

3 ounces bitter chocolate

1/2 cup butter

Combine and stir to melt chocolate. Stir into chocolate mixture:

2 cups sugar

1 teaspoon vanilla

2 egg yolks

*1 teaspoon baking soda, stirred into 1/2
    cup sour cream*

2 cups less 2 tablespoons flour

1 teaspoon baking powder

Pour batter into a well greased and floured 10" tube pan. Bake at 350° for 45 minutes. Cool for 15 minutes, remove from pan and let cool completely. Split cake in half and spread with 10 ounce jar of rasperry or apricot jam.

Frost with following:

2 tablespoons butter

3/4 cup semi-sweet chocolate chips, melted

6 tablespoons whipping cream

1 1/4 cups confectioner's sugar

1 teaspoon vanilla

Beat all together adding more sugar or cream to get desired consistency.

God does not send us strange flowers every year.

When the spring winds blow o'er the pleasant places

The same dear things lift up the same fair faces;

The Violet is here.

ADELINE D. T. WHITNEY
1861

TO REMOVE A STUMP:

Plant hostas as close as possible around a big stump you want to remove. Big hosta leaves shade the stump and keep it moist, hastening the rotting process.

SUNDIAL©

Integrate this sundial into a grandmothers flower garden quilt. Make the sundial metal gray, brassy gold, verdigris green and copper orange.

For a quick mortar for a brick walkway or patio, sprinkle with a cement and sand mixture, sweep into spaces between bricks and hose down lightly.

11

12

13

14

15

16

17

18

19

20

One to rot,
one to grow,
One for the pigeon,
one for the crow

OLD ENGLISH
PLANTING RHYME

21

22

23

24

25

26

27

28

29

30

A woman lost us Eden, such as she alone restore it.

JOHN GREENLEAF WHITTIER

GARDEN TULIP

Tulips come in almost every color of the rainbow except true blue. Defy mother nature and make your tulips blue.

CHEDDAR SOUP

3 tablespoons butter

1 cup chopped onions

1 cup chopped celery

1 cup chopped green pepper

1 cup chopped carrot

Broccoli, mushrooms, spinach or other
vegetables, can be leftovers

1/2 cup cream

3 cups chicken or vegetable stock

1 1/2 cups beer

3 1/2 cups milk

1 to 1 1/2 lbs. grated Cheddar cheese

2/3 cup flour

Sauté onion in butter. Add remaining chopped vegetables, cover and cook until tender. Stir in flour. Add left-over vegetables and stock. Bring to a boil and cook until thickened.

In a separate saucepan heat 3 1/2 cups milk, gradually add the cheese, a little at a time until melted. Combine milk and cheese mixture gradually with the vegetable mixture. Add beer and cream. Heat but do not boil. Makes 10 servings.

DIPPING CROUTONS

Cut day old sliced bread horizontally into four pieces. Crush a clove of garlic and put it into several tablespoons of olive oil. Let stand a few hours. Brush the oil on the bread, on a cookie sheet. Bake 375° until lightly browned and crisp. Watch carefully so they don't burn.

CRAZY QUILT SALAD

1/2 pound spinach

1 cup each of broccoli, cauliflower and
mushrooms, cut into bite size pieces

1/2 cup diced sweet red pepper

3 tablespoons oil

3 tablespoons red wine vinegar

1 finely minced clove of garlic

2 teaspoons Dijon mustard

1/2 teaspoon salt

Dash of pepper

1/2 teaspoon sugar

Combine dressing ingredients, pour over broccoli, cauliflower, mushrooms and red pepper, let stand for about an hour. Just before serving toss in spinach leaves. Garnish with sliced hard cooked eggs and halved cherry tomatoes.

APRIL SHOWERS LUNCHEON

- Cheddar Soup

- Dipping Croutons

- Crazy Quilt Salad

Warm Applesauce

- Cinnamon Cookies

A perfect menu created for a cool rainy spring day. Keep in mind that April Showers bring May flowers. Be patient.

Cinnamon Cookies

3/4 cup butter

1/2 cup sugar

3 1/2 teaspoons cinnamon

2 egg yolks

1 3/4 cups flour

1/4 teaspoon salt

Cream butter, sugar, and cinnamon.
Stir in egg yolks. Stir in flour and salt.
Form into a 14" long log. Chill one hour.
Cut in 1/4" slices, place on lightly greased
cookie sheet. Bake for 17 minutes. Roll
warm cookies in a mixture of 1 cup
powdered sugar and 2 teaspoons cinnamon.

Date Krispies

1 stick butter

1 8-ounce package chopped dates

1 cup brown sugar

Stir together over low heat until melted.
Remove from heat and add:

1 cup Rice Krispies

1 cup chopped nut meats

1/2 cup flaked coconut

Shape into balls or press into 9" x 13" pan.
Dust with confectioner's sugar. Do not bake.

Mint Tea

Rinse freshly picked mint and pack as
much as you can get into a large saucepan.
Cover with water and bring to a boil.
Remove from heat and let stand until cool.
Strain. Add sugar to taste. Serve chilled
with a sprig of mint.

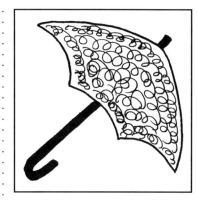

Umbrella

A shower of shimmering
colors will bring a smile to
your face. Then you won't
need an umbrella.

*Ask for a perennial from a
loved one so that every year
when the plant comes up you
will think of that person.*

CHIVE VINEGAR
. . . .

The Vinegar turns a pretty
light pink and takes on a
delicate onion flavor. Heat
white wine vinegar to boiling,
pour over chive blossoms.
Cool and bottle. Leave
blossoms in vinegar.

May

1

2

3

4

5

6

7

8

9

10

To protect seedlings from cutworms use old cat-food or tuna-fish can with both ends cut out. Slip over the seedlings and push half way into the soil.

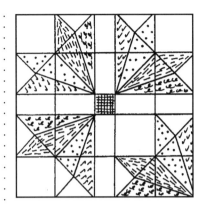

DIANTHUS©

Graduated shades of pink will spice up this variation of the "pink." Leaves should be a grayed blue-green.

QUILTING
•
COOKING
•
GARDENING

Quilting and cooking
Go hand in hand.

I practice each daily
You do understand...?

That both are a science
And I've got 'em down pat.

My quilt pile grows higher
While my body grows fat.

So I've taken up gardening
Not a lot–just a bit.

In a futile attempt
To keep somewhat fit.

The exercise helps
And the veggies are great.

My quilt pile grows slower
But I'm losing weight.

NANCY ROAN

PATCHWORK

I planted a patch of Hollyhocks
Close by the Peony beds,
Where the stately Tiger Lilies
Stand tall and nod their heads.
Around my garden
Is a Rose of Sharon border,
Crossed by paths of Rolling Stones
To keep it all in order.
There behind the picket fence
Where Morning Glories grow,
A stand of Princess Feather
puts on first rate show.
By the Corner Post is a Rambling Rose
With Daisies at its feet.
Not far away are strawberries bright
Red and oh, so sweet.

The Currants and the Cockscomb,
From Grandmother's Flower Garden
Grow there with fragrant lilies
And primrose from seeds I sow.
A bed of Full Blown Tulips
Is edged with Hen and Chicks.
The Cocklebur and Prickly Pear
Need special gardening tricks.
Cactus Flowers, Lotus Flowers,
And golden Sunflowers, too,
Close by Painted Daises
And an Iris of heavenly blue.
Without a single piece of cloth,
Without needles, pins or thread,
I've made a special patchwork quilt
just for my flower bed.

NANCY ROAN

THE MERRY MONTH OF MAY

. . . . .

- **Shrimp and Chicken Jambalaya**

- **Herbed Green Beans**

- **Chocolate Ice Cream Lady Finger Pie**

Don't let Merry May slip by. Enjoy this delightful month before the heat of summer and before the weeds become an overwhelming challenge.

Cut thistles in May,
they grow in a day;

Cut them in June,
that is too soon;

Cut them in July,
then they die.

TRADITIONAL RHYME

SHRIMP AND CHICKEN JAMBALAYA

3 lbs. shrimp

1 lb. smoked sausage

1 lb. chicken breast, cooked

2 tablespoons oil

1 tablespoon butter

1 cup onions, chopped

1 cup green peppers, chopped

1/2 cup celery, finely chopped

1 16 oz. can tomatoes

3 cloves garlic, chopped

1/4 cup fresh parsley, chopped

2 cups chicken stock

1/2 cup green onions, chopped

2 bay leaves

1 teaspoon thyme

1 teaspoon basil

1/8 teaspoon cayenne pepper

1 teaspoon salt

1/8 teaspoon cloves

1/8 teaspoon allspice

1/2 teaspoon chili powder

1 1/2 cups long grain rice

Peel the shrimp. Dice or slice the sausage and sauté in the oil and butter over low heat for 5 minutes. Add the onions, green peppers, celery and garlic and sauté slowly until the vegetables are tender. Stir in the tomatoes, seasonings, rice and stock. Add the shrimp and bring to a boil. Reduce the heat and cover. Simmer for about 25 minutes or until rice is fluffy. During the last 5 minutes of cooking add the green onions and the chopped parsley.

HERBED GREEN BEANS

1 tablespoon butter

1 pint green beans, cooked and drained

1 teaspoon savory

1/s teaspoon oregano

1/s teaspoon basil

1/s teaspoon garlic powder

Melt butter, add beans and herbs. Toss gently and cook till heated through.

CHOCOLATE ICE CREAM LADY FINGER PIE

1 pkg. of 12 lady fingers

2 Bars Baker's German Sweet Chocolate

1/2 cup sugar

4 tablespoon water

4 eggs, separated

1 teaspoon vanilla

1 quart vanilla ice cream, softened

Line 9" pie plate with half of lady-fingers, flat side up - melt chocolate bars (save two squares for grating later) in top of double boiler with 4 tablespoons of water and sugar, until smooth. Beat egg yolks, add to chocolate mixture. Cook for three or four minutes, stirring constantly. Remove from heat, stir in vanilla. Beat egg whites stiff, then fold into chocolate mixture, and spread over lady fingers in pie plate. Arrange remaining lady fingers on top, and cool until firm. Spread softened ice cream over lady fingers, and grate a little chocolate on top. Cover with foil and freeze until firm. Remove from freezer a few minutes before serving. May be served with whipped cream and a chocolate butterfly.

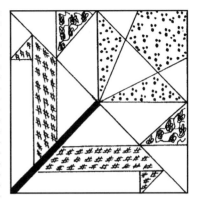

IRIS

The iris is sometimes referred to as "goddess of the rainbow."

N o two men see the same iris.

A.S. BYATT
BORN 1936

Plant Yarrow, Morning Glory, Goldenrod, Nasturtiums, and Marigolds to attract insects to eat aphids and other pests.

11

12

13

14

15

16

17

18

19

20

Earth laughs in flowers

RALPH WALDO EMERSON

PEONY MEDALLION

JODY CLEMENS
74" X 74"

An old fashioned quilt pattern based on a flower prevalent in old gardens delights us in a quilt full of new-fashioned charm.

BUSY DAY IN THE GARDEN

- **Chicken Reuben**

Mini Corn Muffins

- **Garden Lettuce Salad**

- **Ida's Carrot Cake**

- **Mrs. K's Rhubarb Pie**

This is an easy make-ahead dinner for a day when the garden demands your attention. Bake the cake when you have time and freeze it. Buy the muffins!

CHICKEN REUBEN

8 boneless, skinless chicken breast halves

1 16-ounce can sauerkraut

4 slices Swiss cheese

1 bottle Thousand Island dressing

Place chicken breasts in greased 9" x 12" baking pan in one layer. Do not crowd. Tuck ends under to make meat bundles. Sprinkle chicken with black pepper. Drain sauerkraut then spread it evenly over chicken. Cover with cheese slices and pour dressing over the cheese. Cover with foil and bake at 325° for 1 1/2 hours. Remove foil the last few minutes to allow meat to brown.

MRS. K'S RHUBARB PIE

1 1/2 to 2 cups sugar

3 tablespoons flour

1/4 teaspoon salt

2 eggs, beaten

3 cups fresh rhubarb, cut up

1 9" unbaked pie crust

Combine sugar, flour, salt and eggs. Stir in rhubarb. Pour into pie crust. Bake at 450° for 10 minutes then reduce heat to 350° and bake about 30 minutes longer.

GARDEN LETTUCE SALAD

3 cups washed, dried and coarsely cut up garden lettuce

2 diced hard cook eggs

1/4 cup sliced scallions

1/4 cup cream

2 tablespoons sugar

1 tablespoon cider vinegar

Salt and pepper

Place lettuce in serving dish, add eggs and scallions. Combine remaining ingredients, pour over lettuce. Toss just before serving.

IDA'S CARROT CAKE

2 cups sifted flour

2 teaspoons baking powder

1 1/2 teaspoons baking soda

2 teaspoons cinnamon

2 cups sugar

1 1/2 cups salad oil

4 eggs

2 cups finely grated carrots

1 8 1/2 oz. can crushed pineapple, drained

1/2 cup pecans

1 3 1/2 oz. can flaked coconut

Sift flour, baking powder, soda, and cinnamon. Mix sugar, oil, eggs (Beat 2 minutes). Add carrots, nuts, pineapple, and coconut. Pour into greased, floured tube pan or 13" x 9" pan. Bake at 350° for 35-40 minutes. Do not open door first 25 minutes.

CREAM CHEESE ICING

1/2 cup margarine

1 8 oz. pkg cream cheese

1 teaspoon vanilla

1 lb. confectioner's sugar

DANDELION WINE

6 quarts dandelion blossoms

4 quarts boiling water

Pour boiling water over blossoms in a large pot. Let stand for three days and three nights. Strain. Then add:

4 lbs. white sugar

3 sliced oranges

3 sliced lemons

2 tablespoons dry yeast dissolved in 1/4 cup warm water.

Let stand four days and four nights. Strain. Put in glass jugs, fill to the very top. Cover with a piece of glass to keep air out. Add water or excess wine. It can be bottled when it stops working in 2 to 3 weeks depending on the temperature. The old wine makers say "it gets good around Christmas."

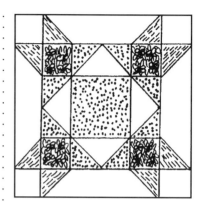

COTTAGE GARDEN

Use the colors you think best reflect the charm of old fashioned English country gardens.

One is nearer God's heart
in a Garden

Than anywhere else on earth.

DOROTHY FRANCES GURNEY

Give fools their gold
and knaves their power;

Let fortune's bubbles
rise and fall;

Who sows a field,
or trains a flower,

Or plants a tree
is more than all.

JOHN GREENLEAF WHITTIER

Big doesn't
necessarily mean
better
Sunflowers aren't
better than violets

EDNA FERBER
(1887-1909)

21

22

23

24

25

26

27

28

29

30/31

Now 'tis spring and weeds
are shallow-rooted;
Suffer them now and they'll
o'ergrow the garden.

WILLIAM SHAKESPEARE
(1554-1616)

STARRY SKY

Select a deep rich blue for the evening sky and make the stars as brilliant and colorful as your fabric stock allows.

There are seashells in my garden. Put a ring of shells around a little seedling you don't want to weed by mistake, or around a perennial that disappears so you don't dig it up by mistake.

Cauliflower is nothing but cabbage with a college education.

MARK TWAIN

1

2

3

4

5

6

7

8

9

10

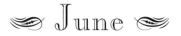
GRASSELAND CHICKEN

3 cups cooked chicken breast cut-up

1 cup fine cut celery

1 cup cooked rice

1 cup drained and sliced water chestnuts

3/4 cup mayonnaise

1 teaspoon salt, lemon juice,
 chopped onions

3 hard cooked eggs, chopped

1 cup cream chicken soup, not diluted

Mix together in casserole & cover with
topping

TOPPING:

1 stick butter

1 cup crushed corn flakes

1/2 cup slivered almonds

Bake at 350° for 30-35 minutes

HERB AND CRUMB TOPPED BAKED TOMATOES

2 tablespoons extra-virgin olive oil,
 plus extra for oiling pan

4 large tomatoes, cored, each cut into
 3-thick slices

4 large leaves fresh basil

1 stem fresh Italian parsley

1 teaspoon fresh thyme leaves

1 teaspoon fresh oregano leaves

1 clove garlic

1 cup coarse bread crumbs, made from
 4 slices day-old Italian bread

Salt, freshly ground pepper

Lightly brush a large baking pan with olive oil. Arrange tomato slices, cut side up, in single layer. Finely chop together basil, parsley, thyme, oregano, and garlic. Combine bread crumbs and half of herb and garlic mixture in bowl. Add 1 tablespoon olive oil and salt and pepper to taste. Toss to blend. Sprinkle tops of tomatoes with crumb mixture, distributing evenly. Bake at 375° until crumbs are lightly browned, about 25 minutes. Transfer tomatoes to large platter. Sprinkle with remaining herb and garlic mixture and drizzle lightly with remaining 1 tablespoon olive oil. Serve warm or at room temperature. Makes 4 servings.

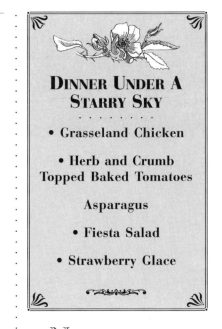

DINNER UNDER A STARRY SKY

- Grasseland Chicken

- Herb and Crumb Topped Baked Tomatoes

Asparagus

- Fiesta Salad

- Strawberry Glace

Now that the earth is warming and the days are getting longer, outdoor entertaining is the thing. Despair not if the skies aren't bright. This menu will be just as tasty indoors.

Tell you what I like the best-
Long about knee-deep
in June,
Bout the time strawberries
melt
On the vine, - some afternoon
Like to jes' git out and rest,
and not work at nothin' else.

JAMES WHITCOMB RILEY
1949-1986

FIESTA SALAD

1 pkg. snowpeas or petite peas,
   frozen fresh

2 large tomatoes chopped or chunked

1 sweet onion sliced or scallions

1 8-oz. mushrooms diced or quartered

1 15-oz. can artichoke hearts, drained
   and quartered

1 small fennel bulb sliced

DRESSING:

1/4 cup olive oil

1/4 cup salad oil

1/4 cup tarragon white wine vinegar

2 teaspoons finely shredded lemon peel

1 tablespoon lemon juice

1 teaspoon sugar

1 teaspoon dried basil crushed

Combine vegetables in large bowl. Set aside.
Combine dressing ingredients in jar cover
and shake well. Pour dressing over
vegetables. Refrigerate for several hours
before serving. When ready to serve, add
romaine, red leaf, spinach or your choice of
lettuces. Toss gently. Add fresh ground
pepper.

STRAWBERRY GLACE

6 cups strawberries

1 cup sugar

3 tablespoons cornstarch

1/2 cup water

1 3-oz. pkg. cream cheese

1 9" inch baked pie shell

Mash enough strawberries to measure 1 cup.
Mix sugar and cornstarch in saucepan, stir
in strawberries and water gradually. Cook
over medium heat, stirring constantly until
thick, then cook one minute. Beat cream
cheese and spread over pie shell, fill with
remaining strawberries. Top with cooked
mixture and refrigerate until set (at least
three hours).

11

12

13

14

15

16

17

18

19

20

This rule in gardening ne'er forget. To sow dry and set wet.

ENGLISH PROVERBS
BY JOHN RAY,
1627-1705

STRAWBERRY JAM

Delicious on biscuits; if you should have some left from brunch.

In a large saucepan put 3 cups cleaned strawberries and 1 cup sugar, cook 5 minutes. Add 1 cup sugar, cook 5 minutes. Add 1 cup sugar, and cook 5 minutes. Pour into a mixing bowl. Cover, let sit overnight. In the morning put into freezer containers and freeze. Will keep a few weeks in refrigerator without freezing.

SHORTCAKE BRUNCH

Orange Grapefruit Juice

• **Strawberry Shortcake**

• **Sausage Patties**
and/or
Crispy Bacon Curls

• **Overnight Coffee Cake**
or
• **Baked French Toast**

Strawberry Shortcake goes front and center for this easy summer brunch. Serve the shortcake in large bowls with milk or (if you dare) cream. No Strawberries? Substitute with delicious and easy French toast.

STRAWBERRY SHORTCAKE

1 cup flour

1 tablespoon sugar

1 1/2 teaspoons baking powder

4 tablespoons butter

1/3 to 1/2 cup milk

Combine dry ingredients, cut in butter, then stir in enough milk to make a dough. Knead a few times on a floured surface. Divide into 4 portions. Pat each into a flat 1" high cake. Place on a greased baking sheet. Brush with butter and sprinkle with sugar. Bake at 450° for 12 to 15 minutes.

Prepare at least one pint of berries by slicing and sugaring, adding the juice of 1/2 lemon. ONLY FRESH WILL DO. Split shortcakes and berries. Replace top of shortcake and top with additional berries. Be generous with berries.

I worked real hard throughout the day
my hands are dirty from earthen clay
my shoes are scuffed, my gloves are torn
My jeans are looking rather worn

MICHELLE GARRETT

SAUSAGE PATTIES

1 lb. fresh pork, ground

1 tablespoon ground coriander

1 teaspoon salt

1/2 teaspoon pepper

Form into 8 patties & sauté until thoroughly cooked.

Think of any of the following flowers to add to your salads:

Anise hyssop

Chive Blossoms

Calendula

Basil

Nasturtium

Violet

Johnny-Jump-Up

Cilantro

Marigold

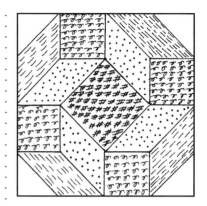

OVERNIGHT COFFEE CAKE

3/4 cup butter

1 1/2 cups sugar

2 eggs, beaten

8 oz. sour cream

2 cups flour

1 teaspoon baking powder

1 teaspoon baking soda

1/2 teaspoon salt

1 teaspoon nutmeg

1 teaspoon vanilla

TOPPING:

3/4 cup brown sugar

1/2 cup walnuts

1 teaspoon cinnamon

Cream butter and sugar. Add eggs and sour cream. Combine next five ingredients, stir into batter, then add vanilla. Mix well. Pour into greased and floured 9" x 13" pan. Add topping. Cover and chill overnight. The next morning, allow pan to stand at room temperature for 15 minutes. Bake in 350° oven for 35-40 minutes.

BAKED FRENCH TOAST

1/2 cup butter

3/4 cup brown sugar

2 tablespoons pancake syrup

1 loaf French, Italian, or Raisin bread

6 eggs

1 1/2 cups milk

1 1/2 teaspoons vanilla

Cinnamon (if desired)

Melt butter, stir in sugar and syrup and stir until all is melted. Pour into a 9" x 13" pan. Place sliced bread in layers on top of syrup in pan. Beat eggs, milk, and vanilla, pour over bread. Sprinkle with cinnamon. Cover and refrigerate overnight. Uncover and bake at 350° for 45 minutes.

Serve with fresh fruit and additional syrup if anyone desires.

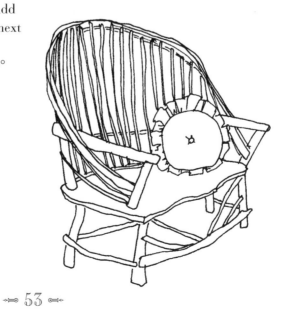

BACHELOR'S BUTTONS

Color this bachelor's puzzle block a variety of blues to make a bachelor button bloom.

The buttercup catches the sun in its chalice

JAMES RUSSELL LOWELL
(1819-1891)

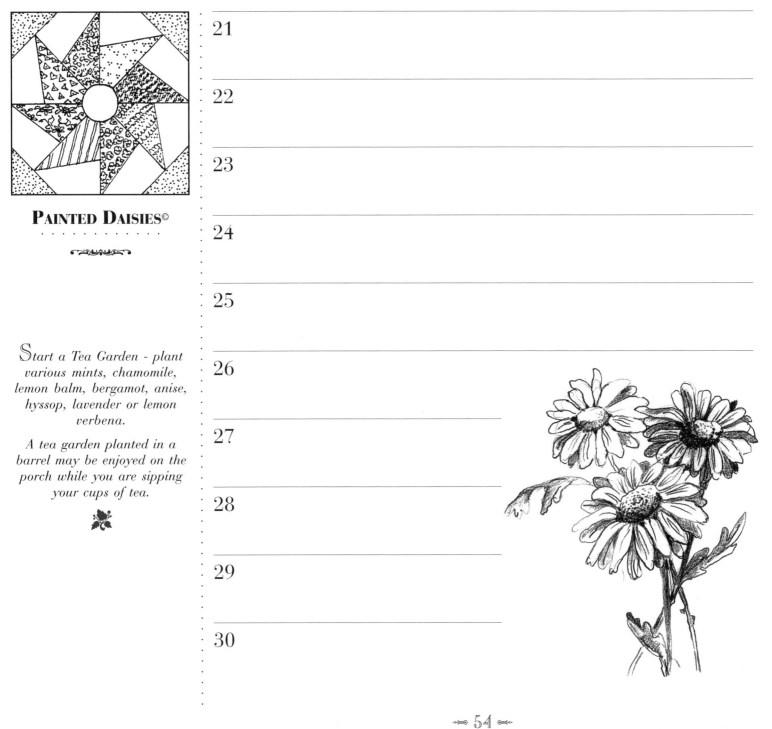

PAINTED DAISIES©

Start a Tea Garden - plant various mints, chamomile, lemon balm, bergamot, anise, hyssop, lavender or lemon verbena.

A tea garden planted in a barrel may be enjoyed on the porch while you are sipping your cups of tea.

21

22

23

24

25

26

27

28

29

30

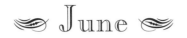

PAINTED DAISIES

KATHLEEN SHAW
82" x 90"

Thoughts of summer make us yearn for a patch of graceful painted daisies. This colorful garden in cloth could satisfy our longings until summer warms the earth.

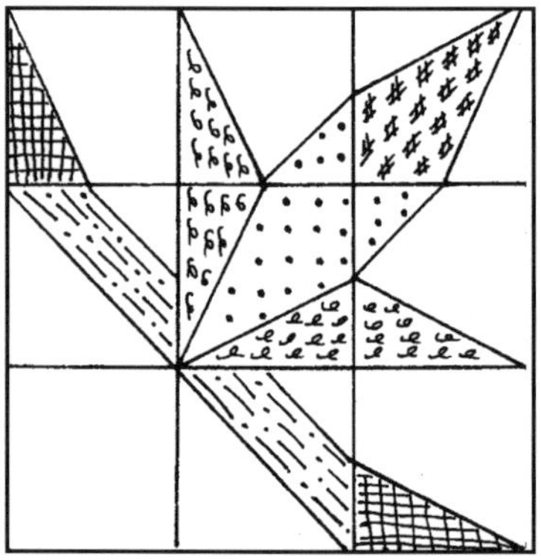

LILIES OF BELLE REVE

Bumble, Bramble,
which came first, sir,

Eggs or chickens?
Who can tell?

I'll never believe that the
first egg burst, sir,

Before its mother
was out of her shell.

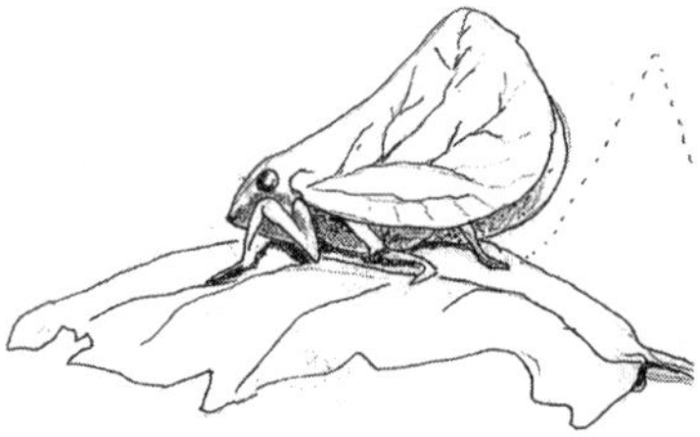

1

2

3

4

5

6

7

8

9

10

A good garden
may have some
weeds.

PROVERB

LILIES OF BELLE REVE

FAY ANN GRIDER
92" x 92"

A neighbor's day lily garden provided the inspiration for this dazzling quilt. Further inspiration from Doreen Speckmann's "Pattern Play - Creating Your Own Quilt" was all this quilter needed. See the results.

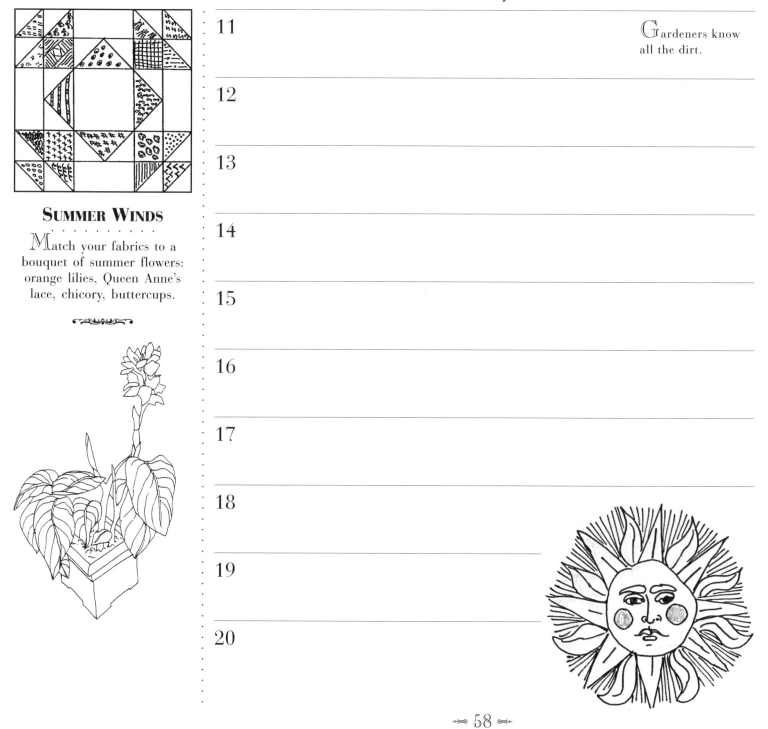

SUMMER WINDS

Match your fabrics to a bouquet of summer flowers: orange lilies, Queen Anne's lace, chicory, buttercups.

11

Gardeners know all the dirt.

12

13

14

15

16

17

18

19

20

CARL'S GRILLED SHRIMP

2 pounds medium or large shrimp, shelled and deveined

2 cloves garlic, minced

¾ cup chopped onion

2 tablespoons fresh parsley, finely minced

½ teaspoon dry mustard

½ cup oil

Juice of one lemon

¼ teaspoon finely grated lemon peel

Marinate shrimp for 1 to 2 hours in the refrigerator. Stir occasionally. Thread shrimp onto skewer. Make sure shrimp are flat by inserting skewer through tail end as well as head end. Grill, basting with marinade and turning frequently, about 10 minutes. Scallops also work well in this recipe.

CRUNCHY WATERCRESS

2 large bunches watercress

1 bunch red radishes

1 teaspoon french Dijon mustard

2 tablespoons wine vinegar or lemon juice

5 tablespoons olive oil

Salt and pepper

Wash and dry watercress. Remove heavy stems. Shred radishes and combine with watercress. Toss with combined remaining ingredients just before serving. Garnish with lemon wedges.

ZUCCHINI BOATS

Select small (5") zucchini. Cut horizontally. Steam upside down for about 5 minutes. Remove to shallow casserole. Sprinkle with garlic, slat, pepper and top with sliced cheddar cheese. Broil until lightly browned.

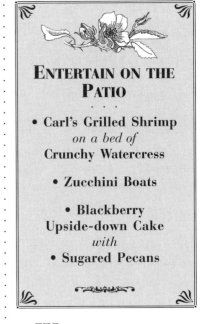

ENTERTAIN ON THE PATIO

- **Carl's Grilled Shrimp** *on a bed of* **Crunchy Watercress**

- **Zucchini Boats**

- **Blackberry Upside-down Cake** *with*
- **Sugared Pecans**

When the zucchini are coming bumper to bumper, watch them carefully and pick before they develop into war clubs.

CAT NIP MICE

Gather cat nip leaves when plants are dry. Spread on cookie sheets to dry thoroughly. It takes a lot, so gather plenty. When dry, stuff cat toys. Your cat won't give a whoop about the shape. Just make it sturdy. Stitch twice, turn, stuff firmly, sew shut securely. Do the stuffing while kitty is having a siesta - preferably in the next county or you'll have the kind of help that impedes progress. Store cat nip and toys in a jar or tin. Do *NOT* hang on the Christmas tree.

BLACKBERRY UPSIDE-DOWN CAKE

1 1/2 cups butter

2/3 cup brown sugar

3 pints blackberries

2 cups flour

1 1/2 cups sugar

3 teaspoons baking powder

1/2 teaspoon salt

6 tablespoons shortening

1 cup milk

2 eggs

2 teaspoons vanilla

Melt butter in a 12" x 9" pan, sprinkle with brown sugar then blackberries. (If berries are frozen, place pan in oven a few minutes to thaw. The cake will bake in shorter time).

Mix batter by combining dry ingredients in bowl. Stir in remaining ingredients, beat until smooth. Pour over fruit in pan. Bake at 350° for 45 minutes. Check center of cake to test for doneness. Bake longer if raw batter sticks to tester.

SUGARED PECANS

2 cups pecan halves

2 tablespoons butter

2 egg whites

1/4 teaspoon salt

6 tablespoons sugar

3/4 teaspoon cinnamon

Place pecans in a baking sheet with sides. Toast in oven at 250° for about 15 minutes. Watch carefully so they don't burn. Remove from oven, add butter, stir to coat nuts. Beat egg whites with remaining ingredients. Pour over pecans and spread to cover. Bake at 250° for about 1/2 hour, watching carefully. Stir to separate nuts. Bake until brown and dry.

PENNSYLVANIA DUTCH APPLE TART

Sprinkle a 9" pie crust with 2 tablespoons sugar and 1 tablespoon flour. Peel and cut in halves enough Lodi or yellow transparent apples to fill the pie crust. (Some turn halves rounded side up, others prefer cut side up) Sprinkle apples with 2/3 cup sugar, 1 tablespoon flour, and 1 teaspoon cinnamon. Pour 1/4 cup cream over pie. Dot with 2 or 3 tablespoons butter. Bake at 375° for about 40 minutes or until apples are soft.

Other apples can be used, but these early apples have a tartness that makes a special pie.

BIRTHDAY CELEBRATION

- Bill's Mom's Frogmore Stew

- Summer Bruschetta

- Spirited Potato Salad

- Lemonade

- Summertime Peach Pie

The "Stew" requires only a minimum amount of time in the kitchen, so it is perfect for hot weather and perfect for eating outdoors. Once the birthday person tastes the peach pie, he'll never miss the cake. Candles on the pie are optional.

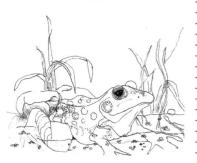

BILL'S MOM'S FROGMORE STEW

This recipe, so easy to fix, is a southern dish and excellent for a summer dinner when the temperature is 95° degrees in the shade. Spread the picnic table with newspapers, lay out the paper plates, lots of napkins and get ready to indulge. For 8 servings:

1/4 cup Shrimp/Crab Boil seasoning

**2 lbs. hot smoked sausage, cut into two" pieces*

12 ears of freshly shucked corn on the cob, broken into about 4" pieces

4 lbs. large fresh shrimp, unpeeled

In stockpot, combine the Shrimp/Crab Boil with 6 quarts of water and bring to a boil. Add the sausage and boil for five minutes. Add the corn and cook for 5 minutes longer. Add the shrimp to the pot and cook until pink and firm and the corn is crisp-tender, about 3 to 5 minutes. Drain immediately and serve.

*If hot smoked sausage is not available, Kielbasa can be used and add 1/2 teaspoon of crushed hot red pepper per serving to the pot.

SUMMERTIME BRUSCHETTA

4 pounds plum tomatoes

8 cloves garlic, finely minced

1/2 cup fresh basil, chopped

1/2 cup fresh parsley, chopped

3 tablespoons lemon juice

Salt and pepper

Sprinkling of crushed pepper flakes

Sliced Italian or French bread

3 or 4 crushed cloves of garlic

1/2 cup olive oil

Scald tomatoes, cool in cold water. Peel and chop coarsely. Place tomatoes and remaining ingredients in a large bowl. Refrigerate for several hours.

Brush bread slices with olive oil. Bake at 350° until crisp. Serve tomatoes in a bowl surrounded by toast.

SPIRITED POTATO SALAD

2 tablespoons vinegar

1 teaspoon celery seed

1 teaspoon mustard seed

Combine and set aside. Pare, cube, and cook 4-6 medium potatoes. When potatoes are chilled, mix:

2 teaspoons sugar

1/2 teaspoon salt

Sprinkle over warm potatoes along with above mixture & chill. When potatoes are chilled, add:

2 cups shredded cabbage

1 12-oz. can corned beef

1/4 cup chopped dill pickle

1/4 cup sliced green onion

Toss with mayonnaise mixture of:

1 cup mayonnaise or salad dressing

1/4 cup milk

1/2 teaspoon salt

LEMONADE

1 cup sugar

3 quarts water

4 lemons

1/2 teaspoon vanilla

1/4 cup orange juice concentrate

Remove yellow rind from one lemon with zester, or remove with knife & sliver. Add rind to sugar and juice of the lemons, concentrate and vanilla. Let stand one hour. Add water and ice and serve. You may want to strain out peel. Makes about 12 cups.

SUMMERTIME PEACH PIE

4 cups sliced ripe fresh peaches

1 tablespoon lemon juice

1/4 cup sugar

3 tablespoons cornstarch

1 tablespoon butter

1/4 teaspoon almond extract

1 9" baked pastry shell

Sprinkle peaches with lemon juice and sugar. Let stand one hour. Drain, reserving peach juice. Add water to make 1 cup of juice. Add cornstarch to reserved juice. Cook over low heat until mixture thickens, stirring constantly. Remove from heat. Stir in butter, extract and peaches. Pour into cooled pastry shell. Chill. Serve with whipped cream or vanilla ice cream.

NO NONSENSE PIE CRUST

2 1/2 cups all purpose flour

2 tablespoons sugar

2 teaspoon baking powder

1 teaspoon salt

1 cup vegetable shortening

1 egg

1/4 cup buttermilk

Combine dry ingredients, cut in shortening. Beat egg with buttermilk, stir into crumbs with fork until blended. With your hands form into a ball. Divide into two portions, wrap in plastic film. Chill. Roll to fit pie dish. Freeze the flattened balls or the rolled crust in pie dish if desired.

F inish dividing and replanting bearded irises.

D ivide and replant bleeding hearts and Oriental puppies.

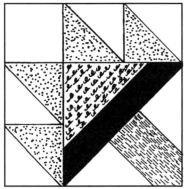

CACTUS FLOWER

Hot and mellow yellows
and prickly greens.
Sew with caution.

Keep cutting annuals, and
fertilize them with fish
emulsion or manure tea to
encourage blooms throughout
the summer. Use manure tea
only once every two to four
weeks and be careful to keep
liquid off the leaves or they
will burn.

21

22

23

24

25

26

27

28

29

30/31

Earth is here so
kind, that just tickle
her with a hoe and
she laughs with a
harvest.

GERROLD
"A LAND OF
PLENTY"

Sow seeds of
pansies and violas
in a shady seed bed
or cold frame.

SUNSHINE AND DAISIES

NORMA GRASSE
72" x 72"

After choosing a hodge podge of favorite fabric scraps to create a field of sunflowers, the design is well tied together with a chain of daisies.

FUCHSIA
. . . . .

Use hot pink and tropical purple to mimic August's temperatures or cool it with pale pink and frosty white. Crisp green leaves are a must.

To promote growth of moss on flower pots or brick surfaces, brush with sour milk or yogurt.

To kill moss on flowerpots or patio, brush surfaces with pine oil

1

2

3

4

5

6

7

8

9

10

Exceptionally hot weather during the first week in August foretells a cold hard winter

TRADITIONAL SAYING

A Gardener's life
Is full of sweets
and sours
He gets the sunshine
When he needs the
Showers

REGINALD ARHELL
(1882-1959)

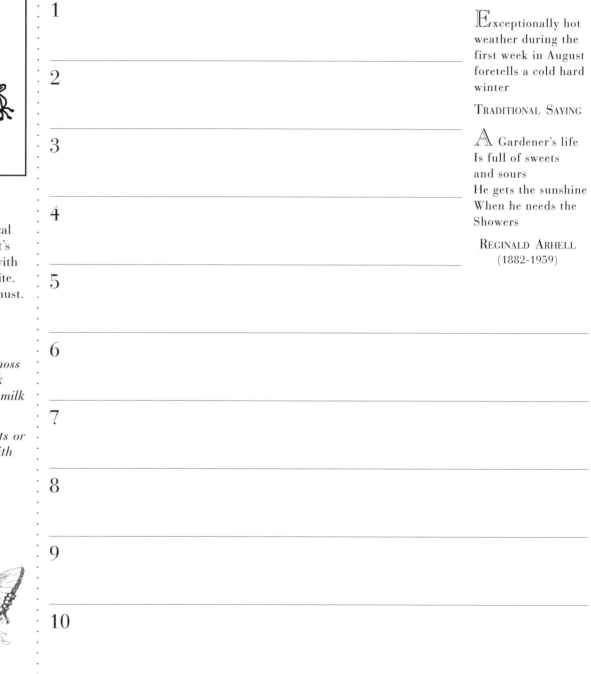

SPECIAL CHERRY TOMATOES

3 dozen cherry tomatoes

1 8-oz pkg. cream cheese

1/2 of a small onion

1/4 teaspoon freshly ground black pepper

4 slices bacon, cooked and crumbled

Several sprigs of parsley

Cut a thin slice from top of cherry tomatoes. Carefully scoop out seeds. Turn upside-down on a paper towel to drain for a few minutes. Chop parsley and onion in food processor, add cream cheese, bacon and pepper, process only till mixed. Fill tomatoes. Garnish with parsley.

CHICKEN SANDWICHES

1 lg. roasting chicken

1/4 cup butter

1/2 cup chopped onion

2 minced garlic cloves

1/4 cup finely chopped onion

Salt and pepper

Thyme, rosemary, & parsley, or your choice

Add herbs, garlic, onion, salt and pepper to soft butter. Spread over chicken. Roast at 350°, basting with butter from pan, until very done. Watch so it doesn't burn. Remove chicken to a cutting board and when cool enough remove meat from bones. Place bones, skin, pan drippings in a stew pot, add one cup water. Cook covered for 1/2 hour then drain and chill broth. Remove fat. Add butter to chicken and heat. If desired, spread onion rolls or pita with some of the solidified butter removed from broth. Taste broth for seasoning before adding to chicken. Place chicken in rolls then wrap the sandwiches in foil and place in a styrofoam chest to keep warm.

There should be just enough broth to moisten chicken. To much will make sandwiches soggy. Broth can be thickened slightly if desired.

SUPPER ON THE BEACH

• **Special Cherry Tomatoes**

• **Chicken Sandwiches**

• **Spinach Squares**

• **Plum Muffins**
with
Streusel

Pack everything in a hamper or the laundry basket to carry to the beach or to poolside. Lacking either of these, opt for the back yard. Don't forget the candles. Votive candles in re-cycled canning jars keep on burning even in a breeze.

SPINACH SQUARES

4 tablespoons butter

3 eggs

³/₄ cup flour

1 cup milk

1 teaspoon salt

2 teaspoon baking powder

1 lb. cheddar cheese grated

*2 boxes chopped spinach,
    thawed and drained*

1 teaspoon onion

Melt butter in 8" square pan. Beat eggs, flour, milk, salt, and baking powder. Mix well, stir in cheese, spinach, and onion. Bake for 35 minutes at 350°. Can be frozen.

D aisies blow
beside the hedges,
White as snow
Along the edges

WARD ANDERSON

PLUM MUFFINS WITH STREUSEL

STREUSEL:

1 cup flour

¹/₂ cup brown sugar

¹/₂ cup pecans, broken

6 tablespoons butter, soft

1 teaspoon cinnamon

Combine to make streusel topping and set aside.

BATTER:

¹/₂ cup butter

³/₄ cup sugar

2 eggs

1 teaspoon vanilla

1 ¹/₄ cups flour

1 teaspoon baking powder

Cream butter and sugar, add eggs, one at a time, add vanilla. Stir in flour, sifted with baking powder, until batter is smooth. Divide batter into greased or lined muffin pans. Arrange 2 or 3 plum slices on each muffin and sprinkle with streusel. Bake at 350° for 25 to 30 minutes.

11

12

13

14

15

16

17

18

19

20

"...Such gardens
are not made by
singing: "Oh, how
beautiful! and
sitting in the shade."

RUDYARD KIPLING

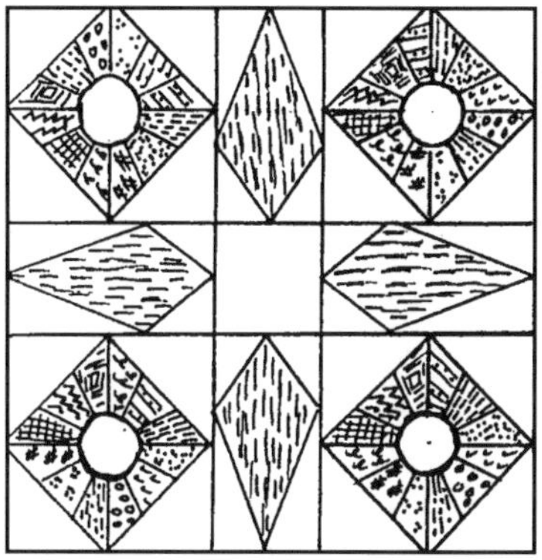

CONEFLOWERS©

CONEFLOWERS©

MARY SHELLY
22 x 22

Designed specifically to
represent a perennial border
favorite. This wall hanging
accomplishes it's intent.
Could it attract butterflies?
Butterfly alert! Over here.

"SUNFLOWER" DIP

*4 lg. yellow bell peppers
(seeded and peeled)*

5 or 6 lg. garlic cloves

1/2 of a medium onion

*2 tablespoons red wine
vinegar*

1 tablespoon olive oil

Salt and pepper later

Tabasco sauce

*1 slice white bread
(crusts removed)*

2 tablespoons sunflower seeds

Broil pepper halves until skin is blackened. Put peppers in a brown paper bag and fold top closed, let stand for 10–12 minutes. Rub off skin.

Place peppers in food processor along with bread, garlic, and onion until the consistency desired. Keep it a bit chunky. Stir in remaining ingredients, season with salt, pepper and additional hot sauce.

Select a large serving plate and a smaller shallow bowl. Place bowl with pepper puree in center of plate. Sprinkle with sunflower seeds. Arrange toasted pita wedges and Belgian endive leaves around bowl petal fashion.

This is low in calories and fat.

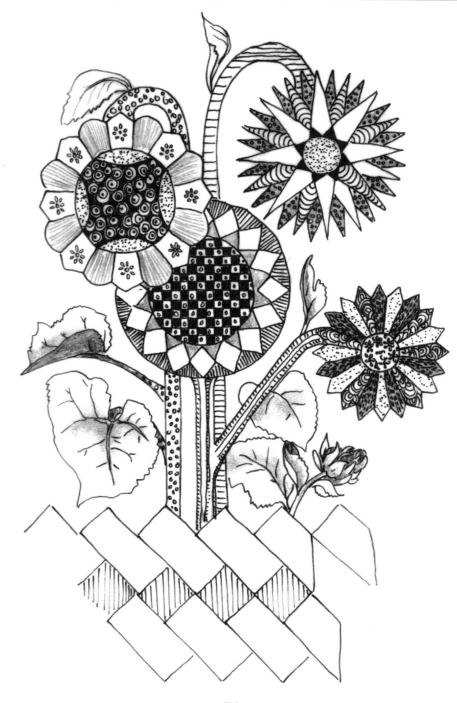

21

22

23

24

25

26

27

28

29

30/31

Children in a family are like flowers in a bouquet... There's always one determined to face in an opposite direction from the way the arranger desires.

We have determined that Sunbonnet Sue has been a gardener for a long time. Why else would she be wearing that Sunbonnet which effectively shields her face from the harmful rays of the sun? Smart girl.

Weeds for Sale– Pick your own

A Bountiful Garden

- **Iced Orange Beet Soup**
  or
- **Gazpacho**

- **Fusilli with Marinated Tomato and Brie**

Crusty Rolls

- **Sour Cream Peach Tart**

Here is a special way to savor the bounty of the garden or roadside stand. Even non-vegetarians will enjoy this menu.

ICED ORANGE BEET SOUP

1 1/2 lbs. beets sliced thin- fresh or canned

1/2 cup chopped onions

1/2 teaspoon dried basil

2 cups chicken stock

1 cup orange juice

Cook onions in microwave - 6 minutes. Combine beets, onions, basil, and chicken stock, simmer over medium heat approximately 15-20 minutes. Cool and puree. Add orange juice and chill. Serves six.

For a festive presentation, put a dollop of yogurt in center of soup and a sprinkle of blueberries. The red, white and blue is all American.

GAZPACHO

2 cups tomato juice

1 beef bouillon cube

2 tablespoons wine vinegar

1 tablespoon salad oil

1/2 teaspoon salt (optional)

1/2 teaspoon Worcestershire sauce

3 drops Tabasco

1 chopped tomato

1/4 cup unpeeled diced cucumber

2 tablespoons chopped green pepper

2 tablespoons chopped onion

Heat tomato juice, add bouillon cube to dissolve. Remove from heat and add remaining ingredients except vegetables. Chill, serve with raw vegetables and herbed croutons.

FUSILLI WITH MARINATED TOMATO AND BRIE

1 lb. fusilli

3/4 lb. brie cheese, chopped into bite-sized pieces

5 or 6 large ripe tomatoes, cut into chunks

1 large clove fresh garlic, crushed

3/4 cup fresh basil, chopped

3/4 cup olive oil

Salt and freshly ground pepper to taste

Marinate all but fusilli at room temperature at least one hour before serving.

Cook fusilli according to package directions. Drain and return to warm pot. Pour marinated mixture over hot noodles and mix together gently. Serve immediately. Six portions.

SOUR CREAM PEACH TART

2/3 cup sugar

2 tablespoons flour

1/4 teaspoon salt

1 cup sour cream

1 tablespoon lemon juice

1/2 teaspoon vanilla

1/2 teaspoon almond extract

1 egg

2 cups sliced peaches (fresh)

1/2 cup brown sugar

1/3 cup flour

1/4 cup butter

Unbaked pastry crust

Beat sugar, flour, salt, sour cream, lemon juice, extract, and egg. Add the sliced peaches; pour mixture into pie crust and sprinkle with cinnamon.

Bake in hot oven (400°) for 25 minutes. Remove from oven and cover evenly within 1/2" of edge with crumbs that have been made by mixing together the brown sugar, 1/3 cup flour and butter. Return to oven and bake 25-30 minutes longer at 350°. This pie is worth the effort and calories.

Who goes out to hoe her garden in the early morning dew?

Faithfully deadheads her zinnias, now I ask you who?

Mulches all her kitchen herbs, asparagus and rue?

Made strawberry jam and baked pies from the berries which she grew?

Reads magazines for quilting and garden manuals too?

Visits her local garden shop for morning glories blue?

Then stops at her favorite fabric store just for a yard or two?

Who grows all the many veggies for a healthy summertime stew?

Who's our favorite quilt block model who likes to garden too?

Sunbonnet Sue

NANCY ROAN

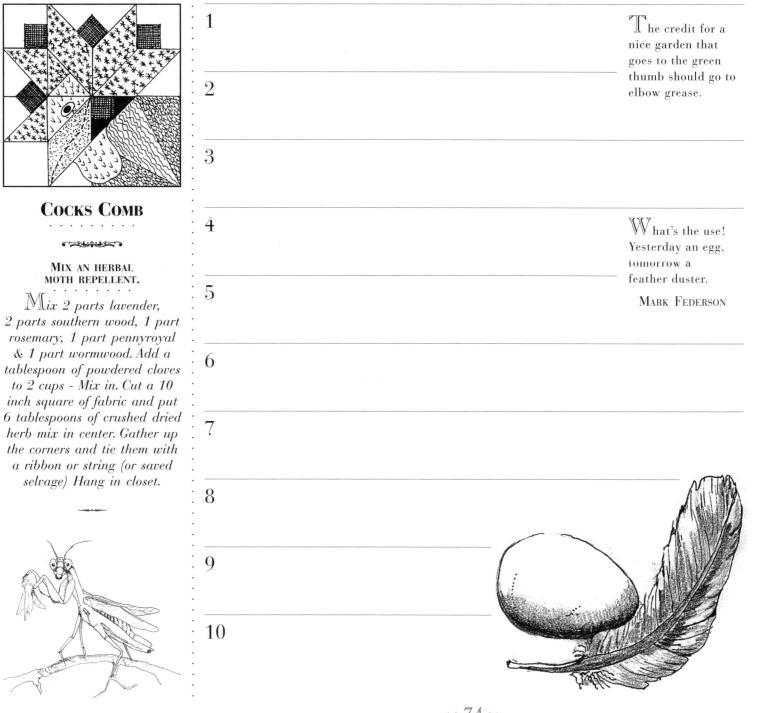

COCKS COMB

**MIX AN HERBAL
MOTH REPELLENT.**

*Mix 2 parts lavender,
2 parts southern wood, 1 part
rosemary, 1 part pennyroyal
& 1 part wormwood. Add a
tablespoon of powdered cloves
to 2 cups - Mix in. Cut a 10
inch square of fabric and put
6 tablespoons of crushed dried
herb mix in center. Gather up
the corners and tie them with
a ribbon or string (or saved
selvage) Hang in closet.*

1

2

3

4

5

6

7

8

9

10

The credit for a
nice garden that
goes to the green
thumb should go to
elbow grease.

What's the use!
Yesterday an egg,
tomorrow a
feather duster.

MARK FEDERSON

COCK-A-DOODLE COCKSCOMB
· · · · · · · · ·
SALLIE ASTHEIMER
86" x 86"

When the maker of this quilt experienced a chicken population explosion in her back yard, it seemed as if the only thing growing in her garden were stately red cockscomb and the "real" cockscombs nesting in the soil.

Sit down to this homey meal and get a full report from the troops on their first day back at the desk. We offer no guarantee, but it would seem likely that this menu could increase homework efficiency.

HAMBURGER POT ROAST

1 lb. ground chuck

1 lb. ground turkey

1/2 teaspoon salt

1/4 teaspoon ground black pepper

1 teaspoon caraway seeds

3 tablespoons milk

1 teaspoon minced garlic

1 large onion, chopped

1 tablespoon olive oil

1/4 cup flour

1/4 teaspoon salt

Dash black pepper

1 teaspoon paprika

2 bay leaves

1/2 cup Burgundy

2 large onions - sliced

Combine meats, 1/2 teaspoon salt, 1/2 teaspoon pepper, caraway seeds, and milk. Sauté garlic and chopped onion in olive oil until light brown. Drain onion and add to meat mixture. Reserve oil and sauté sliced onions in it until they are browned. Add additional oil or butter to frying pan.

Form meat into a 2 to 2 1/2 inch thick patty. Combine flour and remaining salt, pepper, and paprika. Cover meat loaf with flour mixture. Brown on one side, turn carefully to brown other side. Add 2 bay leaves and 1/2 cup burgundy. Reduce heat to very low, Cover and continue to cook turning occasionally until done, about 30 minutes.

Remove bay leaves, cover with the sliced onions, cover and leave on heat to warm onions. For a delicious gravy add 1 cup half and half to pan drippings along with 1/4 cup burgundy, 2 tablespoons lemon juice, and additional salt and pepper as needed. Sprinkle with 1/4 cup finely minced parsley.

CUCUMBER SALAD

4 cucumbers

1 tablespoon salt

1 large onion thinly sliced

1/2 cup sour cream

1/2 cup mayonnaise

1/3 cup sugar

2 tablespoons cider vinegar

Freshly ground black pepper

Peel and slice cucumbers place in a bowl, sprinkle with salt. Let stand at least one hour. Drain and rinse, drain again. Add remaining ingredients. Chill.

SUSAN'S BREAD

2 tablespoons yeast

2 cups warm water

1 cup milk, room temperature

1/3 cup sugar

3 tablespoons butter, melted

1 egg, beaten

8 cups flour, hard wheat

Dissolve yeast in water. Add egg, milk, sugar, melted butter, salt, and 1 cup of flour. Add 2 or 3 additional cups of flour and beat, very hard by hand. This is where the great flavor comes from. Add remaining flour to make a smooth dough. Turn from bowl onto a floured surface and let rest for 10 minutes, then knead at least 10 minutes. Place dough into an oiled bowl, cover with a towel and let rise until double in bulk. Punch down in bowl and divide into three equal portions. Knead each portion lightly to remove air. Let rise again for 10-15 minutes. Roll each piece with rolling pin, into a rectangular shape. Removing all air bubbles. Fold in half length twice. Roll again lengthwise and fold in thirds, place in a greased loaf pan. Cover with a towel and let rise until almost double. Bake at 350° for 30-35 minutes. Remove bread from pans immediately, place on rack and cover with a towel. Cool.

CHOCOLATE STRATA

6 slices firm white bread

2 cups of half and half

2 large eggs

1 teaspoon vanilla

2 tablespoons sugar

2 teaspoons instant coffee dissolved in
  1 tablespoon of hot water

Combine:

1/3 cup cocoa

1/2 cup sugar

Butter slices of white bread, crusts trimmed, place in one layer in buttered dish. Sprinkle with some cocoa/sugar mixture. Add more bread and sugar in layers to fill casserole. Pour egg mixture over bread. Let stand 10 minutes. Place casserole in pan of hot water. Bake at 350° for 40 minutes or until a knife inserted 2 inches from edge of casserole comes out clean. Good warm or chilled, even better with whipped cream.

Sew little pouches from fabric scraps. Fill with seeds saved from your favorite flowers and give to a friend.

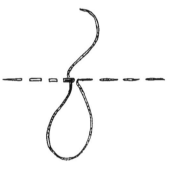

I can complain because rose bushes have thorns or rejoice because thorn bushes have roses. It is all in how you look at it.

L. KINFIELD MORELY

September

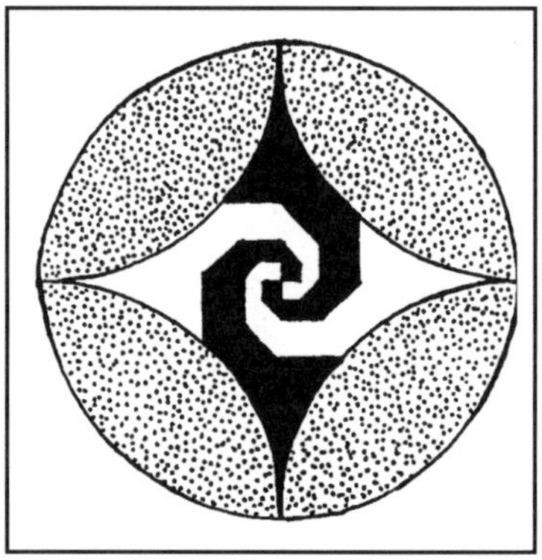

SNAIL TRAIL THROUGH THE MELON PATCH©

Melon colors: yellow, salmon, orange, light green. Snail colors: you're on your own here.

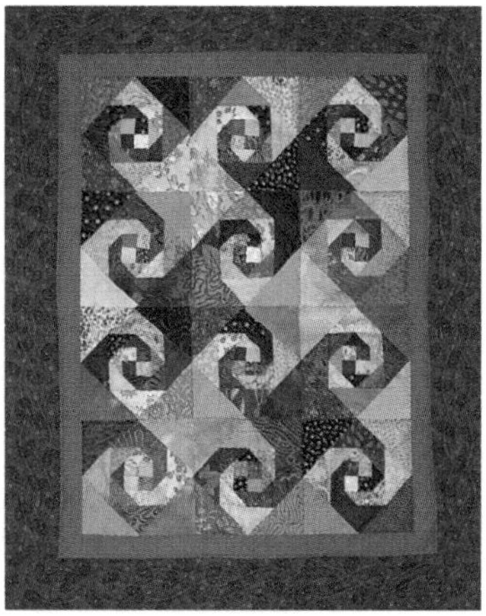

SNAIL TRAIL

MARY SHELLY

Colors inspired by the iridescent trail left behind by a garden dweller. A variation of this traditional pattern is illustrated above.

11

Clear moon, frost soon

FOLK SAYING

12

13

14

15

16

17

18

19

20

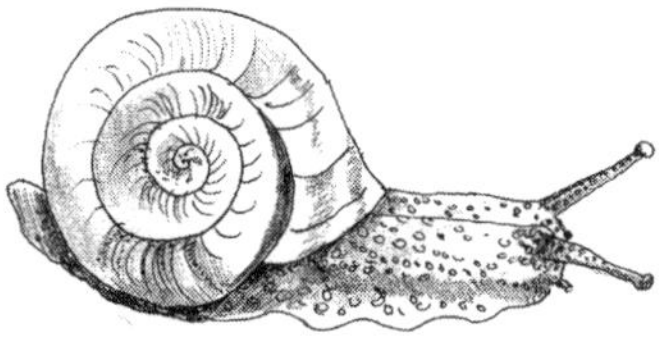

❧ September ❧

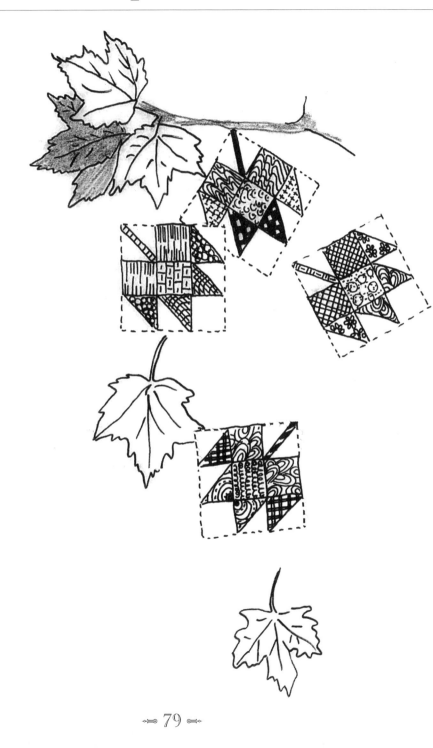

I meant to do
my work today-
But a brown bird sang in the
apple tree, And a butterfly
flitted across the field,
And all the leaves
were calling me.
And the wind went sighing
over the land. Tossing the
grass to and fro and
a rainbow held out its
shinning hand
So what could I do
but laugh and go.

A PENNSYLVANIA DUTCH DINNER

- **Corn Pie**

- **Dutch Tomatoes**

- **Lemon Sponge Pudding**

This dinner is possible only when fresh sweet corn is at its best and when tomatoes are red, ripe, and juicy. No others will do. Plan accordingly.

CORN PIE

4 cups fresh corn

2 chopped hard cooked eggs

Salt and pepper

1 cup milk

2 tablespoons butter

Put corn and other ingredients into pie crust. Cover with top crust. Bake at 400° for 25 minutes or until browned and filling bubbles through slits in top crust. Serve with extra hot milk

Not traditional but good: Make pastry with chilled bacon fat instead of shortening. Add chopped fried bacon to corn. Sausage also is a great addition. Local butcher shops smoke fresh pork sausage.

DUTCH TOMATOES

Slice ripe tomatoes into a deep platter. Add sliced onion. Combine 2 tablespoons brown sugar with 2 tablespoons cider vinegar. Pour over tomatoes. Sprinkle with salt and pepper. Let stand a few minutes before serving.

LEMON SPONGE PUDDING

1 1/4 cups sugar

4 tablespoons flour

4 tablespoons butter, melted

6 tablespoons lemon juice

2 teaspoons lemon rind

4 eggs, separated

2 cups milk

Spray a 2 quart casserole with vegetable spray and set aside. In a large bowl, combine sugar and flour, stir in butter, juice, rind, egg yolks, and milk. Beat egg whites until stiff. Fold in lemon mixture and pour into prepared baking dish. Set dish in pan of hot water. Bake at 350° for one hour.

CORN RELISH

2 quarts corn kernels

1 quart chopped cabbage

1 cup chopped sweet red pepper

1 cup chopped sweet green pepper

1 cup chopped onion

2 teaspoons celery seed

1 teaspoon salt

1 teaspoon turmeric

2 tablespoons dry mustard

2 tablespoons mustard seeds

1 cup water

4 cups cider vinegar

1 1/2 cups granulated sugar

Combine all ingredients, bring to a boil. Simmer for 1/2 hour. Pack into hot sterilized pint size jars leaving 1/8 inch head space. Put on tops. Process for 10 minutes in boiling water bath.

Relish will keep a long time without the hot water bath processing if kept in the refrigerator. Can be made with frozen corn.

A flash of harmless lightning, A mist of rainbow dyes, The burnished sunbeams brightening From flower to flower he flies.

JOHN BANNISTER TALB
"HUMMING BIRD"

HUMMINGBIRD

POTATO CANDY
. . . .

Cook a medium sized peeled potato. Drain well. You can use one from the pot full you've cooked for mashed potatoes, but DO NOT USE LEFTOVER MASHED POTATOES. Mash potato thoroughly, let cool completely but do not refrigerate. Stir in confectioners sugar until the mixture becomes stiff. Give up the spoon and use your hands. Add $1/2$ teaspoon vanilla. Roll candy on a well sugared surface to about $1/4$ inch thick. Spread with peanut butter and rollup as for jelly roll. Slice into $1/4$ inch slices.

21

22

23

24

25

26

27

28

29

30

Count your garden by the flowers that bloom and not by the leaves that fall.

TOASTED PUMPKIN SEEDS

Wash and clean 2 cups seeds. Place in large pot with 3 cups cold water and $1/2$ cup salt. Boil, then simmer and stir until salt is dissolved. Simmer $1/2$ hour. Drain. Spread seeds on cookie tin, bake at 300° for 45 minutes. Stir occasionally. During last 10 minutes break a seed, it should be dry and lightly toasted. Store in jar when cool.

MAPLE LEAVES

Rust, yellow, orange, crimson, burgundy, green. Don't stop with these colors but hurry before they blow away.

No mean woman can cook well for it calls for a light head, a generous spirit, and a large heart.

PAUL GAUGUIN

1

2

3

4

5

6

7

8

9

10

Show me your garden and I shall tell you what you are.

ALFRED AUSTIN
(1835-1913)

Make sure you check over pots and plants that you bring inside for the winter. Mites, ants, and other critters may have taken up residence in the soil.

WRECKED EGGS

1/4 pound loose sweet Italian sausage

Butter or bacon fat

16 eggs

1/3 cup salsa

1 green pepper, chopped

1/4 cup grated Parmesan cheese

Salt and pepper

Sauté sausage in a skillet until thoroughly cooked, breaking it up to keep it crumbly. Set aside. Add butter or bacon fat to a clean skillet. Heat. Beat eggs until light and frothy. Pour eggs into skillet and cook until they begin to set. Stir in remaining ingredients and sausage. Continue cooking and stirring until eggs are cooked.

APPLE CRUMB MUFFINS

2 cups flour

1/4 cup sugar

2 teaspoons baking powder

1/2 teaspoon baking soda

1/2 teaspoon salt

1/3 cup salad oil

1 egg

1 cup buttermilk

1 teaspoon cinnamon

1 1/2 cup finely chopped apple

Crumbs:

1 cup flour

1/2 cup brown sugar

1/4 cup butter or oil

1/2 teaspoon cinnamon

3/4 cup broken pecans or walnuts

In a large bowl, combine flour, sugar, baking powder, soda, and salt. Combine buttermilk, egg, and oil. Mix into dry ingredients stirring only to moisten. At the same time stir in the apples mixed with cinnamon. Divide into 12 greased muffin cups (line with paper liners if you desire). Sprinkle with crumb topping made by combining the crumb ingredients. Bake at 375° for 20 to 25 minutes. Sprinkle with confectioners sugar just before serving.

INDIAN SUMMER BRUNCH

Mixed Melon Balls

• Wrecked Eggs

• Apple Crumb Muffins

October's weather can exhibit both sides of Mother Nature. One day she's like Cinderella's nasty step-mother. The next day she can turn around and display the sweet and sunny disposition of the fairy godmother.
Enjoy her at her best.

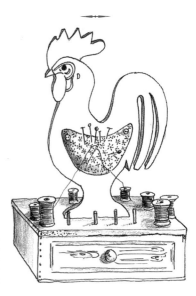

BREAD AND BUTTER PICKLES

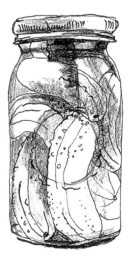

2 quarts sliced cucumbers

1/2 cup salt, not table salt

2 quarts water

6 medium onions, sliced

2 large green peppers, sliced

1 large red pepper, sliced

1 1/2 cups white sugar

1 1/2 cups brown sugar

2 1/2 cups vinegar

1 tablespoon mustard seed

1/2 teaspoon turmeric

1 tablespoon celery seed

Place sliced cucumbers in a glass or pottery bowl. Sprinkle with salt. Add water. Let stand 3 or 4 hours. Drain. Combine remaining ingredients in a large stainless steel pot and bring to a boil. Add cucumbers. Return to a boil, simmer for 5 minutes or until cucumbers are hot. Stir occasionally. Pack in hot jars. Seal. Process in water bath for 10 minutes.

And, as it works, the
industrious bee,

Computes its time
as well as we,

How could such sweet and
wholesome hours

Be reckoned, but with herbs
and flowers.

ANDREW MARVELL
(1621-1678)

CHOCOLATE BUTTERFLY PATTERN

Melt chocolate chips in microwave or over hot water stir in a teaspoonful of vegetable shortening. (Do not use butter or oil). Cut a small corner off of a plastic sandwich bag. Place wax paper on top of butterfly patter. Put chocolate in bag and allow it to flow along butterfly pattern. Chill, then peel paper from chocolate carefully, decorate dessert. Xerox this pattern given here or design your own - try dragonflies or even some fantasy "bug".

11

12

13

14

15

16

17

18

19

20

If the wind comes from the west on October 12th a mild winter follows.

TRADITIONAL SAYING

One Year's seed is seven year's weed

TRADITIONAL RHYME

PUMPKIN PATCH©

What else? Pumpkin orange.

AUTUMN

The morns are meeker than they were,
The nuts are getting brown;
The berry's cheek is plumper,
The rose is out of town.

The maple wears a gayer scarf,
The field a scarlet gown.
Lest I should be old-fashioned,
I'll put a trinket on.

LUNCH AT THE SHORE

- **Crab Spread Appetizer**
- **Toasted Crackers**
- **Taco Soup**

  Grapes

- **Coconut Pound Cake**

W hen the Quilties Ladies spend a weekend at Sea Isle City, good food is important. The cake and components of the soup are made at home minimizing cooking at the shore and allowing more time for quilting or walking on the beach. It's a toss-up whether to work, walk on the beach, or go fabric shopping.

A favorite of the Quiltie Ladies, especially easy and easily transported, this appetizer is always part of our pre-dinner munchies at the shore.

CRAB SPREAD APPETIZER

Place an 8 oz. block of cream cheese on a plate. Top with a can of drained crab meat, then a generous slathering of cocktail sauce. Provide crackers.

TOASTED CRACKERS

1 cup oat flour*

2/3 cup regular flour

1/3 cup wheat germ

1 tablespoon sugar

1 tablespoon sesame seeds

1 teaspoon garlic salt

1/4 cup butter

1/2 cup water

Combine ingredients, cut in butter. Mix in water and shape into a 9" x 1 1/2" log. Chill. Slice very thin, place on ungreased baking sheets. Bake at 375° for about 12 minutes or until they begin to brown.

*Make oat flour by processing 1 1/2 cups rolled oats in food processor for one minute.

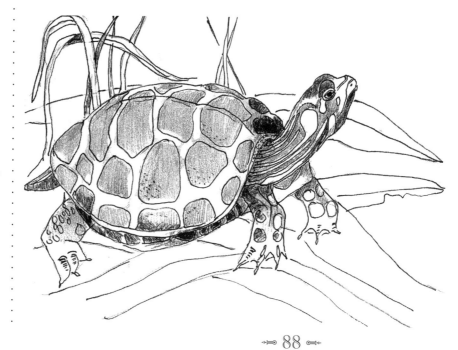

October

TACO SOUP

2 chicken breasts

3 cups water

2 stalks celery

1 onion

2 carrots

2 tablespoons oil

1 tablespoon chili powder

1 tablespoon cumin

1 small can green chilies

1 can chicken broth

1 can beef broth

1 can tomatoes

1 tablespoon Worcestershire sauce

Tortilla chips

Grated Monterey Jack cheese

Cook chicken breast in water until tender. Chop celery & onion. Grate carrots and sauté in oil. Combine all ingredients and simmer a few minutes. Add diced chicken. Top each serving with Tortilla chips and cheese.

COCONUT POUND CAKE

1 pound butter

2 cups sugar

2 cups flour

6 eggs

7 ounces angel flake coconut

1 teaspoon vanilla

Cream butter and sugar. Add 1 cup flour and mix well. Add eggs, one at a time, mixing in well. Mix remaining cup of flour with coconut and add to cake mixture, then mix in vanilla. Place in 9" tube pan. Bake at 350° for one hour to 1 1/4 hour, or until cake begins to pull away from sides of pan. Turn from pan and glaze while hot.

GLAZE:

1 cup sugar

1/2 cup water

1 teaspoon coconut flavoring

While cake is baking, combine glaze ingredients and simmer for ten minutes. Brush onto wrong side of warm cake. Let cool. Best served 24 hours after baking.

Water your perennial beds, during dry periods. Weeds should be pulled and dead flowers trimmed as part of your fall clean up project.

POTS OF BEGONIAS©

"I am interested in innovative design and color, but still want the end result to be more pleasing to the eye than shocking to the soul.

If my work looks traditional to some and contemporary to others, I have achieved the blending of old and new which is my goal."

JANE BLAIR

21

22

23

24

25

26

27

28

29

30/31

POTS OF BEGONIAS©

MARY SHELLY
84" x 98"

A garden party set among pots of begonias on a fellow quilter's patio gave inspiration for these colorful blooms in their terra-cotta pots.

KENILWORTH IVY©

KENILWORTH IVY

MARY SHELLY
14" x 14"

The dainty and delicate Kenilworth Ivy will look as pretty on your quilt as it does on your patio. Try it both places.

1

2

3

4

5

6

7

8

9

10

What is a weed? A plant whose virtues have not yet been discovered.

RALPH WALDO
EMERSON

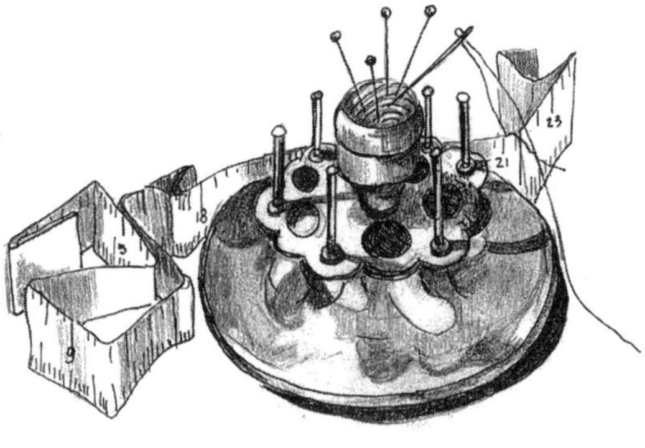

PIONEER GARDEN

. . . .

NANCY COYLE
63" x 65"

Paths of pretty flowers dress up this Log Cabin quilt just as our pioneer ancestors planted flowers to brighten their log cabin gardens.

A BREAK FROM TRADITION

• **Russian Borscht**

• **Orange Glazed Sweet Potatoes**

• **Onion Strata**

• **Potatoes Braised** *in* **Aromatic Broth**

• **Lemon Butter Brussels Sprouts**

• **Sister Mary's Zesty Carrots**

• **Autumn Apple Salad**

• **Lemon Strip Pie**

Surround the traditional turkey with these side dishes. If the gang complains, give in and serve them their sweet potatoes and marshmallows. But, be sure to try these sometime. Be firm about the dessert. They'll forget they ever heard of pumpkin pie. Keep these recipes in mind when you need an idea for a carry-in dinner.

RUSSIAN BORSCHT

1 lb. beef cubes

1 1/2 quart water

1 teaspoon salt

1 1/2 cups shredded raw beets

3/4 cups shredded carrots

3/4 cups shredded turnip

1 medium onion chopped

2 tablespoons tomato puree

2 tablespoons vinegar

1 teaspoon sugar

2 tablespoons butter

1/2 small cabbage shredded

2 bay leaves

Sour cream

Simmer beef. Simmer beets, carrots, turnips, onions, tomato puree, vinegar, sugar, and butter (separate from beef) covered for 15 minutes. Add cabbage and cook 10 minutes longer. Add vegetable mixture, pepper, and bay leaf to meat and broth. Serve with sour cream.

ORANGE-GLAZED SWEET POTATOES

8 medium sweet potatoes cooked and peeled, or 2-1 lb. canned sweet potatoes, drained.

1 cup brown sugar

2 tablespoons cornstarch

1/4 teaspoon salt

1 1/2 cups orange juice

1/2 cup seedless raisins

1/2 cup butter

Shredded orange peel, to taste

Arrange potatoes in shallow baking dish. Sprinkle lightly with salt. In skillet, melt butter, add brown sugar, cornstarch, and orange juice. Simmer until mixture starts to thicken, add 1/2 cup more brown sugar if needed. Stir constantly. Add raisins and orange peel. Pour over sweet potatoes and bake uncovered at 350° for 20 minutes or till potatoes are well glazed. Makes 8 servings.

ONION STRATA

SORT OF A SAVORY ONION BREAD PUDDING

3 cups sliced onions

Sliced white bread

Bacon fat

Salt and pepper

2 1/2 cups milk and half and half mixed

3 eggs

1/2 teaspoon salt

Dash of Tabasco

Bacon

Sauté onions in bacon fat. Layer bread and onions in a shallow casserole greased with bacon fat. Sprinkle with salt and pepper. Combine remaining ingredients, pour over bread and onions. Sprinkle with partially cooked bacon pieces. Place casserole in a pan of hot water. Bake at 350° for one hour. Casserole should puff up. Do not overcook.

POTATOES BRAISED IN AROMATIC BROTH

4 pounds small white potatoes

3 heads garlic, top ¹/₂" sliced off to expose the cloves

3 shallots, unpeeled

4 bay leaves

2 sprigs Italian Parsley

¹/₂ teaspoon white peppercorns

1 ¹/₂ teaspoons kosher salt

3 tablespoons extra virgin olive oil

4 cups chicken broth, homemade or low-sodium canned.

Preheat the oven to 350°. Place the potatoes and garlic in 12" round casserole, at least 3" deep. Scatter the shallots, bay leaves, thyme, parsley, and peppercorns over the top. Sprinkle with the salt and drizzle the olive oil evenly over the top. Pour in the chicken broth. Bake until the potatoes are tender, about 1 ¹/₂ hours. Turn the oven up to 450°. Bake until most but not all of the liquid is absorbed, about 45 minutes longer. Serve, spooning a little of the remaining liquid over the top. Yields: Six servings.

LEMON-BUTTER BRUSSELS SPROUTS

4 packages 10 oz. frozen Brussels Sprouts

¹/₂ cup butter or margarine

¹/₈ teaspoon nutmeg

2 tablespoons fresh lemon juice

¹/₂ of 8 oz. can water chestnuts, drained and sliced

1 small jar drained, chopped pimento

Cook sprouts according to package directions, drain and keep warm in serving dish. Melt butter in saucepan and stir in nutmeg, lemon juice, and chestnuts to warm. Pour over sprouts and sprinkle with chopped pimento. If you prefer, use fresh sprouts cooked. Makes 12 servings.

SISTER MARY'S ZESTY CARROTS

6 carrots

2 tablespoons grated onion

2 tablespoons horseradish

¹/₂ cup mayonnaise

1 teaspoon salt

¹/₄ teaspoon pepper

¹/₄ cup water

¹/₂ cup buttered bread crumbs

Salt

Clean and cut carrots into thin strips. Cook until tender in salted water. Place in 6" x 10" baking dish. Mix together grated onion, horseradish, mayonnaise, salt, pepper, and water. Pour over carrots. Sprinkle with ¹/₂ cup buttered crumbs. Bake about 15 minutes in moderately hot 375° oven. Serves 4 to 6.

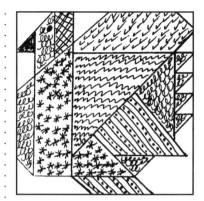

TURKEY HASH©

Nancy Roan

TURKEY HASH

NANCY ROAN
32" x 32"

Tom is elusive. Can he be blamed if Thanksgiving is near? If you can't see him listen for his gobble-gobble.

You can live a long time with a geranium

WINSTON CHURCHILL
(1874-1963)

Turn summer's leftover leggy geraniums into a tree by staking the strongest stem and pruning off all others. Pinch off leaves on the main stem to within a few inches of the top. As the main stem grows, keep pinching off lower side shoots. When the plant is desired height, pinch top to encourage branching.

AUTUMN APPLE SALAD

1 20 oz. can crushed pineapple, undrained

2/3 cup sugar

1 package 3 oz. lemon flavored gelatin

1 package 8 oz. cream cheese, softened

1 cup diced apples

1/2 to 1 cup chopped nuts

1 cup celery

1 cup whipped topping

Lettuce leaves for garnish

In a saucepan, combine pineapple and sugar; bring to a boil, and boil 3 minutes. Add gelatin, stir until dissolved. Add cream cheese; stir until mixture is thoroughly combined. Cool, fold in apples, nuts, celery, and whipped topping. Pour in a 9" square baking pan. Chill until firm. Cut in squares and serve on lettuce leaves. Yield: 9-12 servings

LEMON STRIP PIE

2 tablespoons butter

1 cup sugar

4 tablespoons flour

3 eggs, well beaten

Grated rind and juice of 2 lemons

3/4 cup sweet molasses or dark Karo

1 cup cold water

Combine and cook over low heat until thickened. Cool slightly.

DOUGH STRIPS:

1 cup flour

1/2 cup sugar

Pinch of salt

1 teaspoon baking powder

4 tablespoons butter

3 to 4 tablespoons milk

Mix flour, sugar, salt, and baking powder. Cut in butter. Moisten with just enough milk to hold dough together. Roll on floured surface to 1/4 inch thick, forming a rectangle approximately 6" x 8". Cut into 1/2" strips. Divide the filing into two unbaked pie crusts. Place strips on top, one way only (not crisscross). Bake at 450° for 10 minutes. Reduce heat to 375° and bake for 20 minutes longer until strips are puffed and brown.

CALICO PIE

2 cups diced cooked chicken or turkey

(or for that matter any cook meat)

2 cups seasoned gravy, white sauce or creamed soup - or combination

1 peeled and finely chopped clove of garlic

A bunch of green onions- sliced

1 sweet red pepper - diced

1 cup peas - if fresh - cook briefly, if frozen, thaw

1 cup cooked carrots sliced

1/4 cup chopped parsley

1 tablespoon chopped thyme

1/2 cup sour cream

1 teaspoon Dijon mustard

Sauté onions, garlic, and pepper in 2 tablespoons butter until limp - do not brown. Add to sauce, soup, or gravy. Heat - thicken if necessary. Add remaining ingredients. Pour into a deep casserole. Top with pie crust or biscuits. (yours or purchased). Bake until crust is brown and pie is bubbly. Mushrooms, corn, Brussels sprouts, small onions are other possibilities for adding to this pie.

OZARK PUDDING

4 eggs

2 1/3 cups sugar

1 cup flour

1 3/4 teaspoons baking powder

1/4 teaspoon salt

6 cups chopped apples

1 teaspoon vanilla

1 cup chopped nuts

Beat eggs and sugar until light. Stir in remaining ingredients. Pout into greased 9" x 12" pan. Bake at 350° for 35 to 40 minutes. Serve warm with vanilla ice cream.

CHRISTMAS TREE FIRE RETARDANT RECIPE

2 cups Karo corn syrup

2 ounces chlorine bleach

2 pinches Epson salts

1/2 teaspoon Borax

Fill a 2 gallon bucket with hot water to 1" or 2" below top. Mix ingredients thoroughly. Cut 1" from tree and immerse. Store in protected area until ready to trim. Keep level full daily without exception.

LEFTOVERS UPDATED; THANKSGIVING RECYCLED
. . . . . .
- **Calico Pie**

Cranberry Sauce

- **Ozark Pudding**

Ice Cream

Be flexible about the contents of this pie. It's designed like a scrap quilt, you make from leftovers.

Make your yard more attractive to birds by placing bird feeders and bird baths near protective bushes and trees. Besides offering shelter and nesting sites, many also provide food.

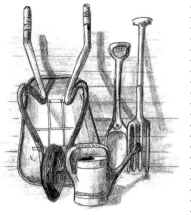

11

12

13

14

15

16

17

18

19

20

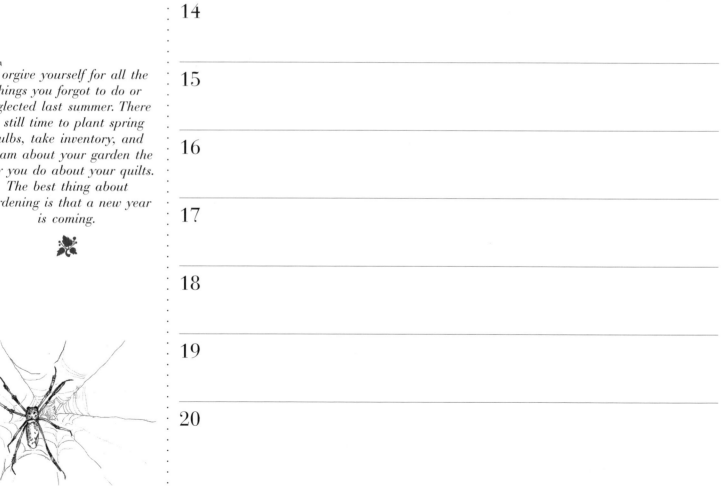

Leaves fall all day long

Quietly singing their quiet song

and every day from dusk to dawn

They fall onto every lawn.

HANNAH SHAW
AGE 9

Forgive yourself for all the things you forgot to do or neglected last summer. There is still time to plant spring bulbs, take inventory, and dream about your garden the way you do about your quilts. The best thing about gardening is that a new year is coming.

Putting the garden to bed. Don't mulch too early because a warm mulch bed is attractive to mice and other rodents who will snack on your plants and plant roots during the winter. Allow the plants to "naturally" go to sleep drawing nutrients into their roots as the soil cools. Provide mulch after the ground is frozen.

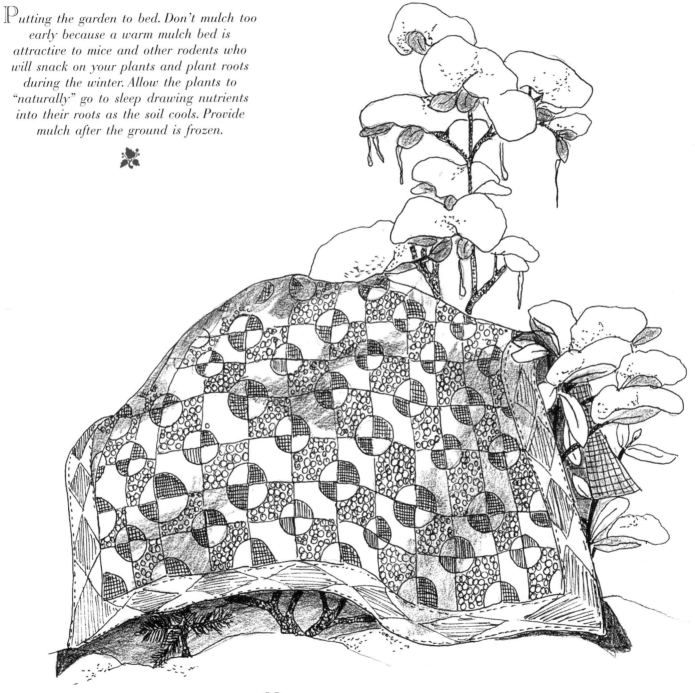

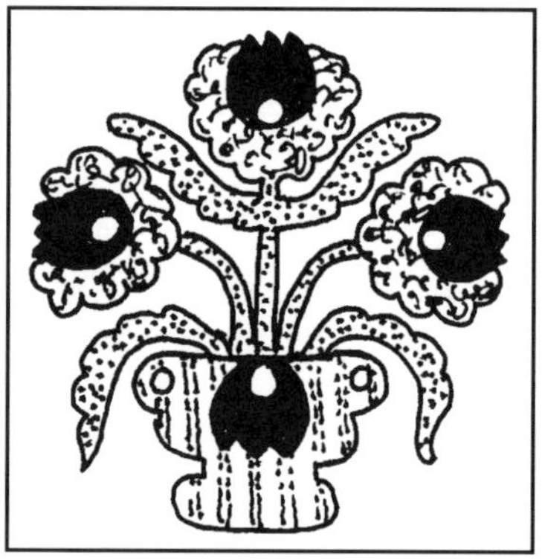

CHINESE CHRYSANTHEMUM©

Primary colors give a
traditional look.
Forget tradition.
Visit your garden center and
look for new color ideas.

"Tis very warm weather
when one's in bed"

JOHNATHAN SWIFT
1667-1745

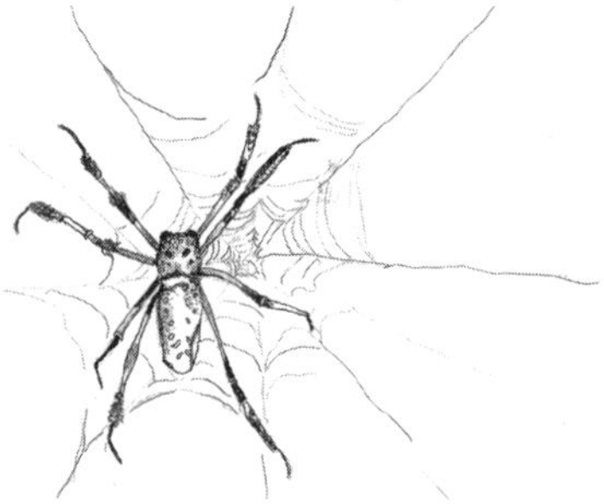

21

22

23

24

25

26

27

28

29

30

Onion skins
very thin
Mild winter
coming in.

Onion skins
very tough
Coming winter
very rough

TRADITIONAL RHYME

ALL SEASON SANTA©

Nancy Roan

SNOW CRYSTALS©
· · · · · · · · · · ·

Any color that catches and
reflects the sunlight or the
moonlight. Remove sunglasses.

*In 1829 in South Carolina,
Jed R. Poinseth, the U.S.
Ambassador to Mexico,
brought home a magnificent
red plant hence the Poinsettia
got its name.*

1

2

3

4

5

6

7

8

9

10

What a pity
flowers can utter
no sound! A singing
rose, a whispering
violet, a murmuring
honeysuckle -
OH, what a rare and
exquisite miracle
would these be!

HENRY WARD
BEECHER
(1818-1887)

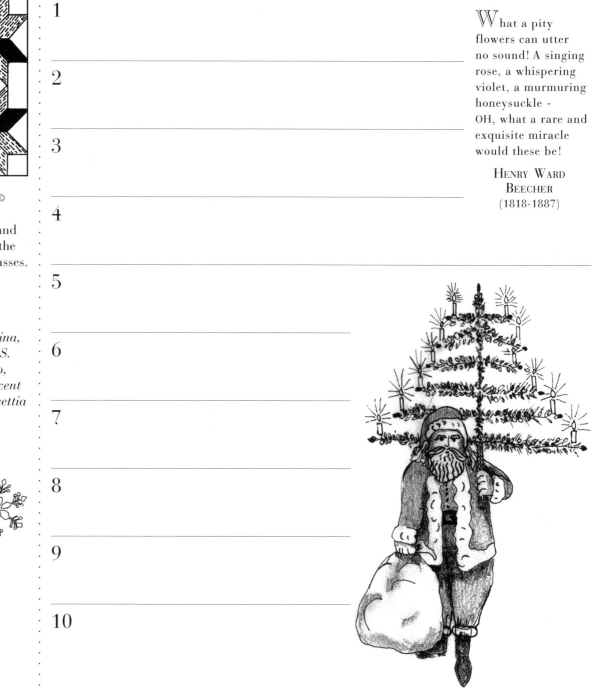

EMERGENCY FAJITAS

1 tablespoon oil

1 lb. boneless chicken breast - cut into thin strips.

1 medium onion - sliced thin

1 red and 1 green pepper thinly sliced

1 clove of garlic - minced or in a pinch, 1 teaspoon bottled minced garlic

1 cup salsa

Heat oil in fry pan. Sauté everything, stirring occasionally until chicken is thoroughly cooked. Add one cup salsa - heat through. Serve on warmed corn tortillas with chopped lettuce, onion, shredded cheese and/or sour cream. Let everybody do their own.

SEAFOOD PIZZA

2 ½ cups flour

¾ teaspoon salt

1 package rapid rise yeast

1 cup warm water

Put dry ingredients in food processor bowl. Add water slowly and process to make dough. Knead and roll out to a 12 inch circle. Place on floured pan. Spread with 1 can seafood bisque, sprinkle with chopped shrimp and crab meat. (Imitation crab is an economical substitute for the real thing). Top with shredded Monterey Jack cheese, chopped fresh tomato and sprinkle with Old Bay Seasoning. Bake at 500° for 12 to 14 minutes. In the summertime peel, seed, and dice tomatoes. Freeze in small quantities to use for this pizza as well as in other dishes.

CHRISTMAS SHOPPING BAILOUT

- **Emergency Fajitas**
  or
- **Seafood Pizza**

Ice Cream

After you've been battling the crowds at the mall, you deserve a break. Eat out. If you must cook, this simple supper should be easy to prepare especially if you get the kids to help. They can shred the lettuce. Don't forget to pick up their favorite ice cream.

If you enjoy the fruit, pluck not the flower.

TRADITIONAL SAYING

COOKIE SWAP

A cookie swap is a way to get a variety of cookies and baking only one or two kinds. For the swap each participant brings a batch of cookies which are then divided among the participants.

Our list gives you numerous options for taking to the swap. If you're ambitious, bake all of them just for yourself.

THE NEEDLE'S EXCELLENCY

Flowers, plants, and fishes, beasts, birds, flies and bees,

Hills, dales, planes, pastures, skies, seas, rivers, trees

There's nothing near at hand or farthest sought

But with the needle may.... be shaped and wrought

JOHN TAYLOR
(1580-1653)

KIFELS

1 pound butter

1 pound cream cheese

6 cups flour

Combine to make dough. Divide into 6 portions. Refrigerate. Roll one portion at a time in confectioners sugar and cut into 3-4" squares. Place a small amount of apricot, lekvar or nut filing in center of each square. Fold dough from opposite corners. Pinch to seal in filling. Bake at 350° for 20 to 25 minutes.

P.B.C.'S

1/2 cup butter

1/2 cup peanuts

1/2 cup sugar

1/2 cup brown sugar

1 egg

1/2 teaspoon vanilla

1 1/4 cups flour

3/4 teaspoon baking soda

1 bag miniature peanut butter cups, unwrapped

Combine all ingredients except peanut butter cups to make dough. Place a ball of dough in each of 48 ungreased small muffin cups. Bake dough for 12 minutes. Remove from oven (one pan at a time). Press a miniature peanut butter cup into center of dough. Let cool in pans. Do not overbake dough. Dough must be hot when adding candy.

CHOCOLATE JUMBLES

4 oz. bitter chocolate (melted)

1/2 cup shortening

8 oz. dark molasses

1/2 cup brown sugar

1/2 teaspoon each of cinnamon, cloves, and allspice

1/4 cup hot coffee

1/4 teaspoon soda

1/2 teaspoon baking powder

1 egg

1/2 teaspoon lemon extract

1/2 teaspoon vanilla

1 3/4 cups flour

Combine all ingredients except flour, stir until well blended. Stir in flour. Drop on greased cookie sheet. Bake at 350° for 12 minutes. Frost cookies with lemon icing.

APES COOKIES

3 eggs

4 cups sugar

3/4 pound butter

1 teaspoon Baking Soda

8 cups flour (approximately)

1 teaspoon vanilla

Cream butter and sugar. Beat in eggs. Add baking soda to flour and mix into butter, sugar and egg mixture. Chill for 2 hours. Roll out and use your favorite cookie cutter. Preheat oven to 350°. Bake 8 to 10 minutes.

11

12

13

14

15

16

17

18

19

20

Make garlands
of yo yos for your
Christmas tree a fun
take along project
for throughout
the year.

FLEUR-DE-YO-YO©

FLEUR DE YO YO

NANCY ROAN
8 1/2" x 8 1/2"

A newly introduced species in
to the plant world the flour de
yo yo comes in a full color
range. While it does have
enemies it is sure to flourish.

A De "Lite" ful Holiday Dinner

• Carrot Soup

• Mushroom Stuffed Chicken Rollups
with
Angel Hair Pasta

Sliced Naval Oranges

• Brownie Sticks

Stuffed from holiday food? Try this low calorie, low fat menu. If you serve this in the summertime, substitute sliced fresh peaches for the oranges.

Happiness is to hold flowers in both hands

JAPANESE PROVERB

CARROT SOUP

1 large onion chopped

1 large clove garlic, minced

1 1/2 cups diced potatoes

2 cups diced carrots

1 can reduced sodium chicken broth

1 tablespoon cornstarch

1 can low fat evaporated milk

1/2 teaspoon nutmeg

1/4 teaspoon pepper

1 teaspoon thyme

1 teaspoon hot pepper sauce

Sauté onion and garlic in a pan sprayed with vegetable oil spray until limp. Cook potatoes and carrots in the chicken broth. Drain, reserve cooking liquid. Puree potatoes, carrots, and onion mixture. Return to cooking liquid and thicken with the cornstarch. Add remaining ingredients. Heat, serve with whole wheat croutons and a spoonful of salsa.

MUSHROOM STUFFED CHICKEN ROLLUPS

2 whole chicken breast

1/2 lb. mushrooms, chopped

1/2 medium onion, finely chopped

For 2 items above coat a non-stick skillet with olive oil spray heat to medium, add onions and mushrooms and white wine. Cook until vegetables wilt and begin to brown and liquid boils away (cover for part of cooking). Cool.

Pound chicken breast to 1/4" thick between sheets of wax paper. Sprinkle with pepper and divide mushroom/onion mixture on the flattened chicken breasts, roll up and secure with wooden toothpicks. Coat clean fry pan with olive oil spray and sauté chicken rolls until lightly brown. Add:

1 cup chicken broth

1/2 cup white wine

Cook for about 10 minutes until chicken is cooked. Remove rolls from skillet - keep warm.

COOK:

4 oz. angel hair pasta toss with 2 table-spoons of chicken broth from skillet, thicken broth with 1 tablespoon flour. Add 1/4 teaspoon dried dill, need simmer for a few minutes. Arrange sliced chicken on top of angel hair pasta. Pour sauce over. Garnish with fresh dill. Sprinkle each serving with a teaspoon freshly grated Parmesan cheese.

BROWNIE STICKS

1/2 cup cocoa

1/3 cup flour

1/2 teaspoon baking powder

6 tablespoons sugar

4 tablespoons brown sugar

1/2 cup egg substitute

2 tablespoons corn oil

2 tablespoons applesauce

1 teaspoon vanilla

Line an 8" x 8" square baking pan with foil - spray with cooking spray. Combine all ingredients and stir until well blended. Spoon into foil lined pan. Bake at 350° for 20 minutes. Cool. Remove from pan by lifting foil. Cut into 16 squares. For a serving cut a square into 4 slices or sticks and serve with fresh peaches. About 80 calories and 4 grams of fat in each 4 sticks.

SPARKLING PUNCH

8 bananas

16 oz. can frozen lemonade concentrate

16 oz. can frozen orange juice concentrate

40 oz. crushed pineapple

1 gallon and 1 1/2 cups water

3 cups sugar

2 two liter gingerale

Combine bananas, concentrates and pineapple. Puree in blender. Add sugar and water. Add gingerale when serving. The fruit mixture can be frozen.

EVANGELINE'S PENNSYLVANIA ROSE©

Cultivate the flowers in red and green. Sew a bed of roses to satisfy your urge to garden in December.

❦

"A quilt is far more than three layers of materials held together by meticulous stitches. For many quilters it is the thread that connects them to others, whether in day to day quilting activities or to stitchers of past generations."

NANCY J. MARTIN

In the name of the bee,

And of the butterfly,

And of the breeze,

Amen

ENVOI BY EMILY DICKINSON
(1830-1836)

Evergreen boughs make a fine shelter for many perennials and shrubs. Cut the branches from your Christmas tree and recycle them in your garden.

21

22

23

24

25

26

27

28

29

30

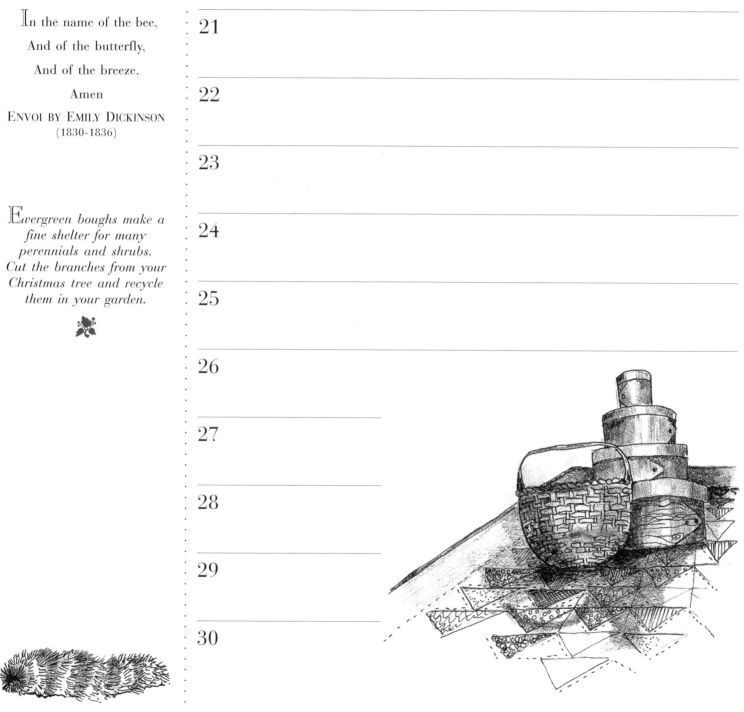

❧ December ❧

I heard the freezing, driving,
winter rain

Rattle like needles on my pane
last night;

When morning broke, the sun
on shrub and tree

Revealed a fairy world
of ice and light;

Each tree once etched so dark
against the sky

Now gleams like some great,
crystal chandelier,

Hung with a thousand prisms
flashing forth

Bright diamond glints that
fade and reappear;

The birches bend in slender,
shining loops,

As iridescent arches
on the snow,

And evergreen are sheathed
in coats of ice

That slant their branches
earthward, drooping low;

I hear the farmers talk of
icy roads

And grounded wires and
damaged sheds and orchards;

I know I should be practical
and sad,

But the sheer, shining beauty
makes me glad.

OLIVE DRIVER

QUILT PATTERNS AND INSTRUCTIONS

GATHERING BASKET

VARIABLE STAR QUILTERS
79 X 83

Designed for a raffle quilt for our 1996 quilt show.
Gathering Basket exhibits the abundance of a flower garden.
The bold striping combined with the floral appliqué produces a striking effect.

ALL SEASON SANTA©
. . . .

Important!! - Santa's face/hats/caps are actual size. - Santa's outfits are 50% and must be enlarged.

Head and face

Add seam allowance to patterns
Cut: A-2 of beard fabric
      B-1 of face fabric

Appliqué face to one A piece - appliqué other features, embroider eyes and mouth. Mustache and eyebrows are of beard fabric. Nose and cheeks are a deeper pink than face.

Sew A's right sides together. Trim and clip. Carefully make a 1 inch slit in back. Turn. Stuff slightly but evenly and quilt. Head must be flat and somewhat stiff. Whip-stitch slit closed.

Background Fabrics

Cut size - 20" x 24 1/2"

PJ's

Cut PJ's, cuffs, hands, teddy bear, and feet. Appliqué to background fabric. Add buttons for decoration. Embroider bear features. Apply head, stitching only at points shown between x's. Sew snaps (3) under beard. Make nightcap. Cut 2 of cap fabric and 2 of lining. Stitch each right sides together. Turn fabric cap, insert lining into cap, turn under lower edge and stitch shut. Make tassel and attach. Cap fits over head.

Santa Suit

Cut suit of red fabric, cut boots and attach. Cut lining identical to entire outfit. Stitch to lining along with thin batting. (Lining should be same color as suit.) Leave neck edge open. Clip and turn in raw edge, whip-stitch shut. Add fur trim (warm & natural cotton batting). Make sack and tree. Attach. Quilt as desired. Quilting helps to flatten and stiffen. Align snaps on neck edge with those under beard. Sew snaps in place.

All hats are made as the night cap. All other outfits are made as the Santa suit. Piece the gardener's shirt and pants as well as the boots before stitching to lining. Sleeves can be cut separately and appliquéd to body of shirts/coats or they can be defined with quilting. We added beads to the snowman "suit" to add a snowy sparkle.

Before binding wall hanging, add a deep pocket on back to store out of season outfits. It should be about 10" deep and go across the entire wall hanging.

Carefully stitch by hand through the center of pocket making two pockets; take care not to allow stitches to show in front.

ALL SEASON SANTA©

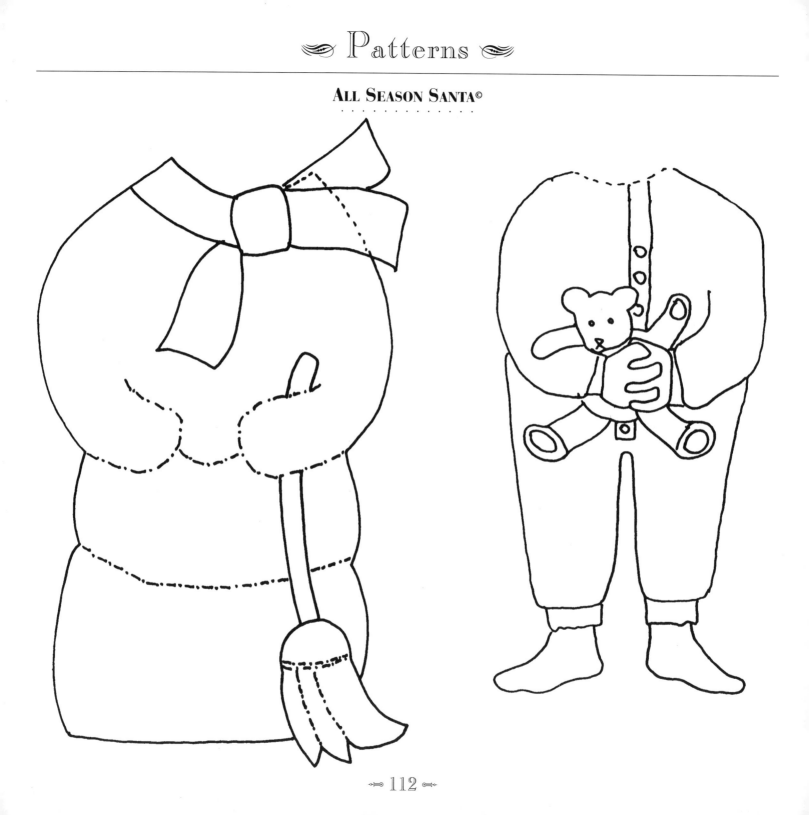

ALL SEASON SANTA©

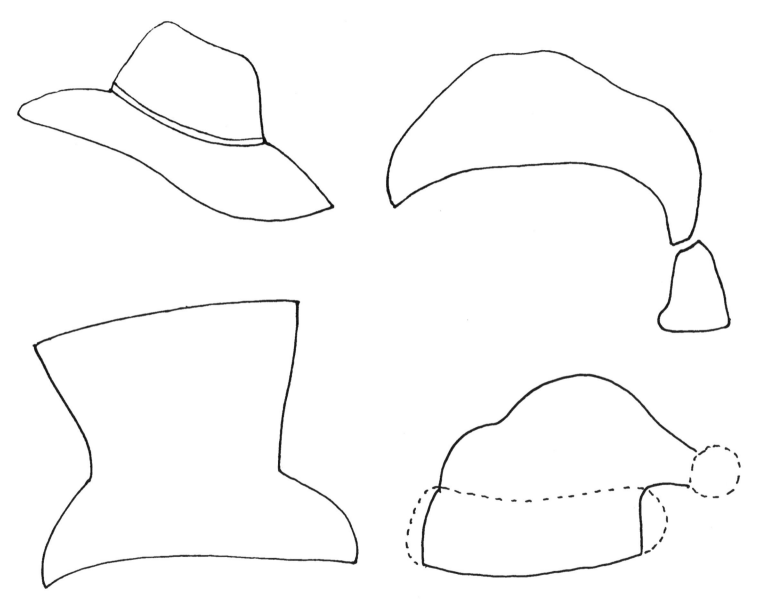

ALL SEASON SANTA©

ALL SEASON SANTA©
. . . .

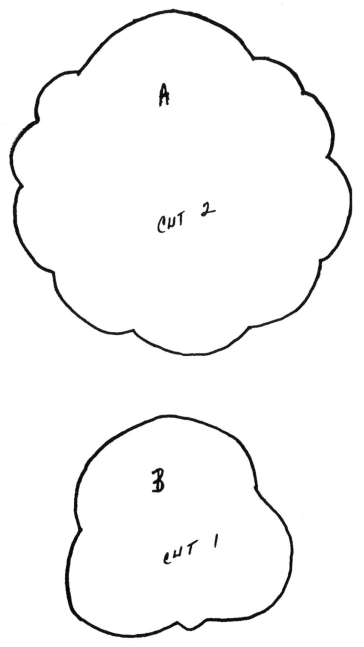

A-Whole outline of beard,
   including top of head

B-Face

Note: Attach to background only
       between x's. This keeps head free
       to put on hats.

OLD NORTH WIND©
· · · · · · · · · · · · · ·

Use Old North Wind as a
quilting design on spacer blocks
of a quilt or just quilt him with
colored thread and frame.

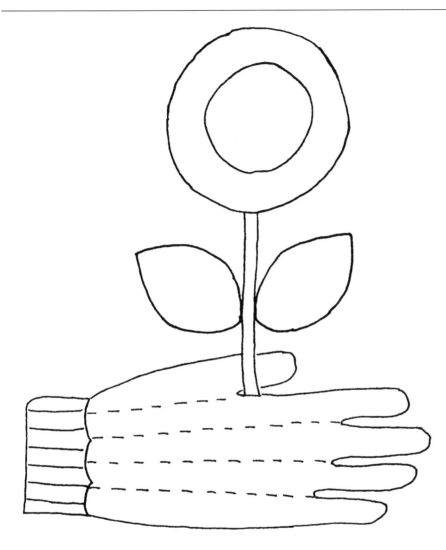

GARDEN GLOVES©

Pattern given is 50% of actual size.

Enlarge to desired size and add 1/4" seam allowance to all templates.

Choose multi-colored flowers and a plain background. Add a butterfly or two, then quilt a bug of your choice on the background. You'll find ideas for "bugs" on various pages of this journal.

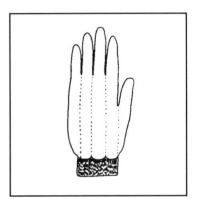

KENILWORTH IVY©

Find a leaf in your garden and replace the ivy leaf. Be creative.

Add ¼" seam allowance to all templates. Pattern shows one-fourth of a 10" block.

Cut:

A 4

B 1

C 4

D 4

D 4 (cut-out).

For cut-out in D, trace opening in center and do in reverse appliqué.

❧ Patterns ❧

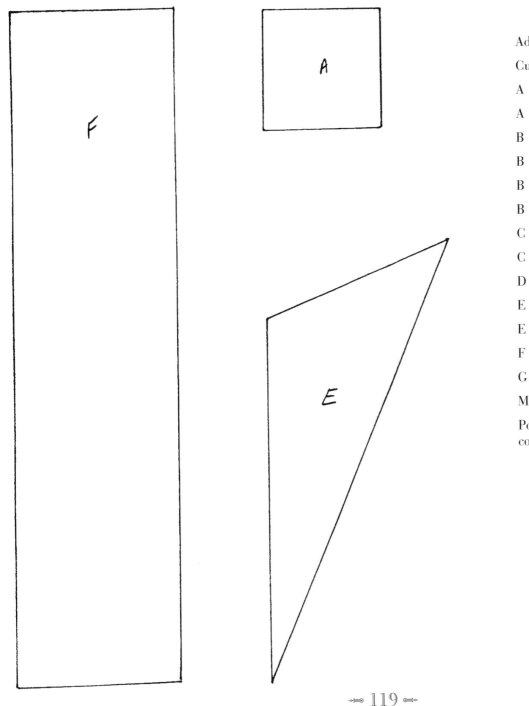

POTS OF BEGONIAS©
· · · · · · · · · · · · · ·

Add ¹/₄" seam allowance to all templates.

Cut:

A 2 color 1

A 2 background

B 2 color 2

B 2 color 3

B 4 color 4 (green leaves)

B 5 background

C 2 color 4 (green leaves)

C 4 background

D 1 color 5

E 1 background

E 1 background (reverse)

F 1 color 6 (flower pot)

G 1 color 6 (flower pot)

Makes 1 - 10" block

Pot up your favorite plants in our terra cotta pots.

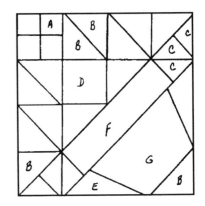

✺ Patterns ✺

POTS OF BEGONIAS©

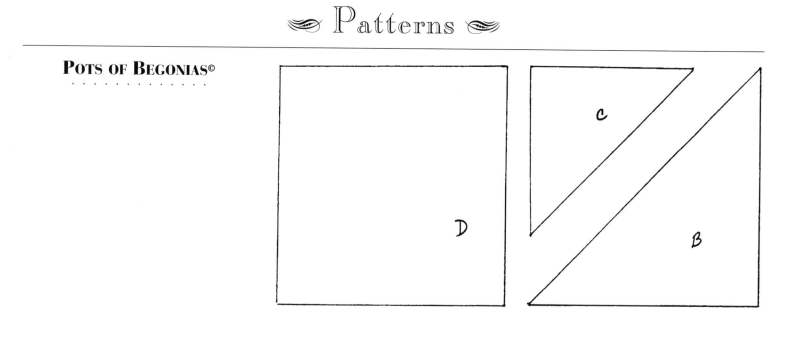

D

C

B

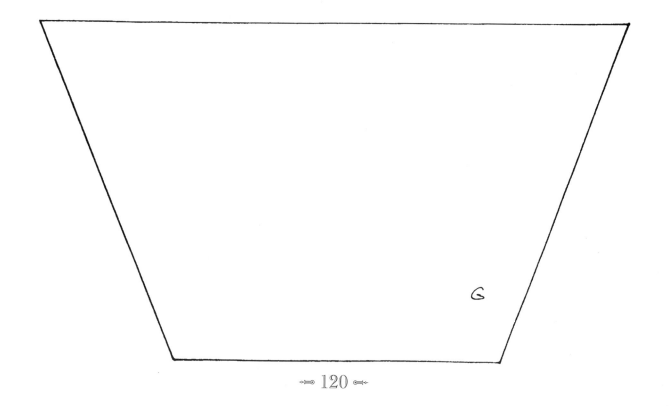

G

SNOWLADY©
. . . .

Pattern given is 70% of actual size.

Enlarge to desired size and add 1/4" seam allowance to all templates.

Add details with embroidery or permanent fabric pen. Find some antique buttons for her dress and give her a paisley scarf. She is very style conscious.

SWEETHEART ROSE©
. . . .

(pictured on cover)

To make a Sweetheart Rose, select two shades of desired color and cut an 18" x 2 ½" strip from each.

Draw an undulating line down the center of one strip on the wrong side (see illustration) with right sides together, stitch along this line, across one end and one long edge. Trim seams, clip curves and corners and turn to right side; press.

Beginning with the raw edge of the strip, roll up and fold until you see a rose taking shape. This may take some experimentation; try folding some edges back for petals. Each rose will be different, just as nature intended.

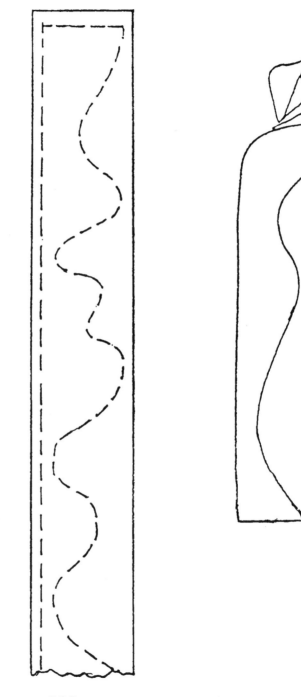

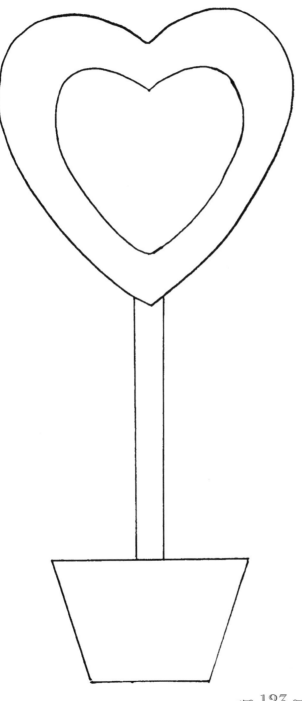

VALENTINE TOPIARY©

Enlarge this until you reach a size you like. Add 1/4" seam allowance to all templates. Cover the heart, broderie perse style, with reds, pinks, and purples if it's for your sweetheart.

Cover a spring topiary with yellow daffodils, pale purple crocus, white snowdrops - whatever you can find blooming at the fabric store.

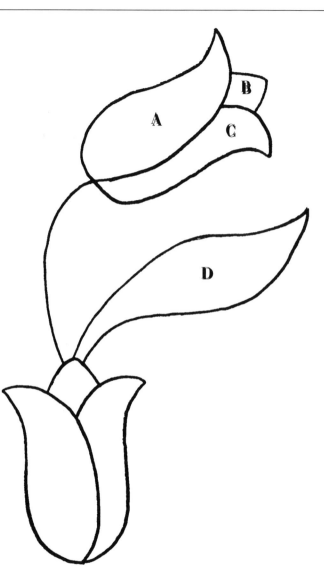

WIND-BLOWN TULIPS

A variation of Wind-Blown Tulips. Tulips constructed of 3 pieces to give flower some dimension.

Add ¼" seam allowance to all templates.

Cut:

A 16 petals

B 16 centers

C 16 petals

D 8 leaves

Appliqué on to a 14 ½" block

Do stems in back-stitch

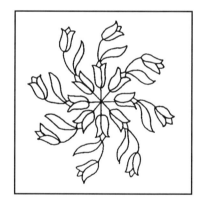

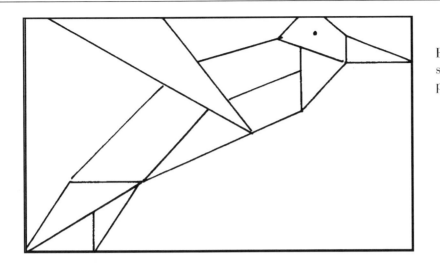

HUMMINGBIRD©

Enlarge drawing to desired size. Add ¼" seam allowance to all templates and piece.

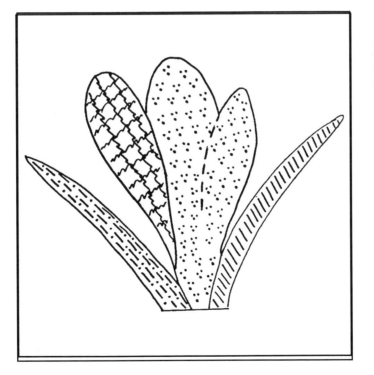

SPRING CROCUS©

Enlarge drawing to desired size. Add ¼" seam allowance to all templates and appliqué.

Index

RECIPES

BEVERAGES

Dandelion Wine 45
Lemonade 63
Mint Tea 35
Sparkling Punch 107

SOUPS

Bean and Pasta Soup 8
Carrot Soup 106
Cheddar Soup 34
Gazpacho 72
Iced Orange Beet Soup 72
Mushroom Onion Soup 16
Russian Borscht 94
Sausage Corn Chowder 12
Taco Soup 89

BREADS

Apple Crumb Muffins 85
Baked French Toast 53
Dipping Croutons 34
Focaccia 12
Overnight Coffee Cake 53
Plum Muffins with Streusel 68
Quick Tomato Herb Loaf 4
Susan's Bread 77

APPETIZERS

Crab Spread Appetizer 88
Lee's Pretzels 10
Mustard Cheese Dip 8
Shrimp Butter Hearts 18
Special Cherry Tomatoes 67
Sunflower Dip 70
Toasted Crackers 88

SALADS

Autumn Apple Salad 96
Crazy Quilt Salad 34
Crunchy Watercress 59
Cucumber Salad 76
Dutch Tomatoes 80
Fiesta Salad 50
Garden Lettuce Salad 44
Spirited Potato Salad 62
Summertime Bruschetta 62
Warm Raspberry Salad 31

MAIN COURSES

CHICKEN

Calico Pie 97
Chicken Sandwich 67
Chicken Puffs 21
Chicken Reuben 44
Chicken Romaine Salad with Honey Mustard
   Dressing 16
Grasseland Chicken 49
Mushroom Stuffed Chicken Roll-ups 106

PORK

Pork Tenderloin Dijon 30
Sausage Patties 52

SEAFOOD

Carl's Grilled Shrimp 59
Frogmore Stew 62
Seafood Pizza 103
Seafood Stew 4
Shrimp and Chicken Jambalaya 40

MISCELLANEOUS

A Good Sandwich 8
Corn Pie 80
Emergency Fajitas 103
Fusilli Salad 5
Fusilli with Marinated Tomato and Brie 73
Hamburger Pot Roast 76
Layered Cabbage Casserole 24
Wrecked Eggs 85

Index

RECIPES

VEGETABLES

Baked Onions Au Grautin 30
Herb and Crumb Topped Baked Tomatoes . 49
Herbed Green Beans 41
Lemon-Butter Brussels Sprouts 95
Mushroom Mousseline 21
Onion Strata 94
Orange Glazed Potatoes 94
Potato Cups 30
Potatoes Braised with Aromatic Broth 95
Sister Mary's Zesty Carrots 95
Spinach Squares 68
Zucchini Boats 59

DESSERTS

Apple Cake 13
Bellefonte Cake 22
Blackberry Upside Down Cake 60
Chocolate Butterfly Pattern 86
Chocolate Ice Cream Lady Finger Pie 41
Chocolate Strata 77
Coconut Pound Cake 89
Cream Cheese Icing 45
Fresh Summertime Peach Pie 63
Hot Caramel Sauce 13
Ida's Carrot Cake 45
Lemon Sponge Pudding 80
Lemon Strip Pie 96
Mad About Chocolate Cake 31
Marble Ricotta Cake 24
Mrs. K's Rhubarb Pie 44
No Nonsense Pie Crust 63
Ozark Pudding 97
Pennsylvania Dutch Apple Tart 60
Sour Cream Peach Tart 73
Strawberry Glace 50
Strawberry Shortcake 52
Vanilla Frozen Custard 17

COOKIES

Apes Cookies 104
Brownie Sticks 107
Cinnamon Cookies 35
Chocolate Jumbles 104
Date Krispies 35
Graham Cracker Brownies 9
Kifels 104
PBC's 104

E.T.C.

Bread and Butter Pickles 86
Catnip Mice 60
Chive Vinegar 36
Corn Relish 81
Easter Eggs 22
Potato Candy 82
Sauerkraut Candy 25
Strawberry Jam 51
Sugared Pecans 60
Toasted Pumpkin Seeds 83
Wild Bird Seed 9

Patterns

QUILTS, PATTERNS, AND BLOCKS

· ·

A

All Season Santa 101, 111–115

B

Bachelor's Buttons 53
Baby Tulip 28
Bleeding Heart 17

C

Cactus Flower 64
Chinese Chrysanthemum 100
Cock-a-doodle Cockscomb 74, 75
Cottage Garden 45
Coneflowers 69
Crimson Rose Valentine 14

D

Dianthus 37

E

Evangeline's Pennsylvania Rose 107

F

Fleur de Yo-Yo 105
Forget -Me-Not 11

G

Garden Gloves 22, 23, 117
Garden Traditions 29
Garden Tulips 33
Gathering Basket 110

H

Hummingbird 81, 125

I

Iris 41

J

J. Everett Nyce and Friends .... Introduction

K

Kenilworth Ivy 92, 118

L

Lilies of Belle Reve 56, 57

M

Maple Leaves 84

O

Old North Wind 116
Old Snowflake 7

P

Painted Daisies 54, 55
Peony Medallion 43
Pioneer Garden 93
Pots of Begonia 91, 119, 120

S

Spring Crocus 26, 125
Snail Trail Through the Melon Patch 78
Snow Crystals 102
Snow Flowers 2, 3
Snow Lady 1, 121
Starry Sky 48
Summer Winds 58
Sundial 32
Sunshine and Daisies 67
Sweetheart Rose 122

T

Turkey Hash 95

U

Umbrella 35

V

Valentine Topiary 14, 123

W

Windblown Tulips 19, 20, 124